78 Days of Terror

Other books by Ken McCarthy

The Nuremberg Code: 75th Anniversary Commemorative Edition, with Vera Sharav

Unraveling the CoVid Con: Vol.1 (The Red Book)

Unraveling the CoVid Con: Vol.2 (The Blue Book)

The System Club Letters

The Nuremberg Code And Its Modern Enemies (Coming 2024)

78 Days of Terror

The US-Led NATO Attack on the Civilians of Yugoslavia

Ken McCarthy

B

Brasscheck
Press

78 Days of Terror: The US-Led Attack on the Civilians of Yugoslavia
by Ken McCarthy

Published by Brasscheck Press

Brasscheck Press
P.O. Box 145
Tivoli, NY
Brasscheck.com

KenMcCarthy.com

Cover design by Taura Hanson

Printed in the United States of America.

"Wars do not usually result from just causes but from pretexts." — General William Tecumseh Sherman

Table of Contents

June, 1999

July, 1999

Preface

This book is an account of a vicious, unprovoked, and unjustified military attack on a civilian population as it unfolded. It was not written retrospectively months or years after the fact with the benefit of time. Each entry was published in immediate response to current events.

Before the Internet, there were four ways to write about war:

1) actually be a war correspondent and accompany troops into battle,

2) hang out in the capital city, far from the action, in a hotel (preferably one with a swimming pool and a well stocked bar), and relay whatever junk information and propaganda your side wants you to deliver,

3) go to press briefings at the Pentagon, write down whatever the spokesperson says, and relay it, uncritically, to the public as fact, or

4) years (or decades) after the war is long over write a dense tome revealing that the war was based on and perpetuated by fraudulent government statements enabled

by inept and/or corrupt news media.

With the Internet, a fifth option emerged: Deconstruct obvious government, military, and mass media lies as they are being delivered.

This fifth approach to war reporting, the book in your hands, was unique in 1999 - and it would still be relatively unique today. The author, Internet commercialization pioneer Ken McCarthy, offered it as a demonstration of how the Internet could be used to report and analyze news, independent of government, military, corporate, or ideological censorship.

The contents of this book are taken from his 1999 blog: www.Brasscheck.com/yugoslavia - where you can also find a detailed index of all the topics covered.

- Paul Morrison, 2022

Introduction

When did American "liberals" go off the track?

In 2022, as I write this, it's pretty clear there is something terribly and drastically wrong with the Democratic Party, and so-called liberals.

Where once the party had been a genuine advocate for social reform - supporting practical issues like labor, civil rights, the environment, and improved access to health care and education - it's now preoccupied with increasingly bizarre and irrational causes, to the detriment of its original mission.

When did liberals go off track?

That would have been in the 1990s when Bill Clinton and his wife Hillary, who was the Democratic candidate for president in 2016, were in the White House.

One of Clinton's earliest acts as president was to preside over the siege and eventual murder of men, women, and children of the Branch Davidian religious community in Waco, Texas. The community had been accused of drug dealing - a charge that later proved to be false - and that accusation created legal conditions that enabled Wesley Clark to provide military equipment from Fort Hood, Texas to "participate" in the siege. (In fact, Clark appears to have overseen the siege and final assault - an assertion I back up with abundant circumstantial evidence in the June 14, 1999 entry: “From Waco to Belgrade: Wesley Clark and America's ‘Army of the Future.’”)

American "Liberals" were untroubled.

Clinton also supervised non-stop attacks on the civilian infrastructure of Iraq - power plants, water systems, manufacturing facilities, schools, hospitals, roads and bridges. When asked if the death toll of Iraqi children from those attacks and the accompanying sanctions, which were estimated to be as high as 500,000, was worth it, Clinton's Secretary of State, Madeleine Albright, answered: "I think that is a very hard choice, but the price, we think is worth it."

American "Liberals" were untroubled.

After the still-inadequately-explained bombing of the Alfred P. Murrah Federal Building in Oklahoma City, in 1995, the Clinton administration gutted due process with the Anti-Terrorism and Effective Death Penalty Act, which was the direct precursor to the PATRIOT Act, another civil rights abomination.

American "Liberals" were untroubled.

The Clinton administration stage-managed the repeal of the Glass-Steagall Act of 1933, a law which reined in some of the worst abuses of Wall Street, namely the use of depositors' money for speculation. What followed was a near-complete breakdown of the stability and integrity of the financial markets, which gets worse with every passing year.

American "Liberals" were untroubled.

The Clinton administration strong-armed the government of Haiti, the poorest country in the western hemisphere, into dropping tariffs on heavily subsidized US-grown rice (much of it from Arkansas) which resulted in the destruction of the island's nearly 200 year old rice-growing infrastructure.

American "Liberals" were untroubled.

The Clinton administration started the movement to put armed police in public schools, creating conditions whereby young children have been handcuffed and charged criminally for simple acts of misbehavior.

American "Liberals" were untroubled.

In 1995 and 1996, Clinton's Secretary of Health and Human Services, Donna Shalala, radically changed the vaccine injury table, thus depriving countless adults and children of compensation for vaccine injuries which previous petitioners had received compensation for as a matter of course. The original laws regarding federal vaccine injury compensation called for "fair, equitable and quick resolution" of cases. Under the Clinton administration, Department of Justice attorneys were instructed to take an extreme adversarial stance against injured petitioners, and to drag out cases as long as possible, with the aim of denying as many claims as possible.

American "Liberals" were untroubled.

Finally, on March 24, 1999, Clinton and fellow Arkanasan and Rhodes Scholar Wesley Clark, under the guise of NATO, began a 78 day terror bombing and murder campaign against Yugoslavian civilians, literally picking up where the Nazis left off in 1941.

American "Liberals" were not only untroubled, they cheered and angrily shouted down anyone who questioned the obviously fraudulent narrative.

This last story is what is covered in this book, which is the complete collection of my blog posts written as this murderous multi-month assault was taking place.

March, 1999

Early Warning

Distress message from a Yugoslavian civilian

March 27, 1999

The targets in the assault on Yugoslavia appear to be similar to those singled out during the assaults on Iraq in the 1990s and Nicaragua in the 1980s (not to mention the mini-assault on Sudan last year): basic economic and social service infrastructure.

Note the attack on the Yugo factory. That's one way for the US-German auto industry to remain competitive, isn't it?

The voices you don't hear:

***

Forwarded message:

Date: Sat, 27 Mar 1999 08:35:20 -0800 (PST)

Tijana Mirovic wrote:

Dear friends,

This has gone too far!!! It is an unbelievable outrage!!! Yesterday we were sitting in our shelters listening to bombs destroying our city and our people! For those of you who still don't know what to think about these aggressions I will share some of the information that we got:

- yesterday they bombed 17 spots in Belgrade! Amongst them : A HOSPITAL 4 SCHOOLS, A FACTORY WITH TOXIC MATERIAL (which got spilled and jeoperdized the lives of all civilians living in that area). And let me tell you that in that same area not far from that factory there is a home for mentaly deprived children (children with Down sindrome, cerebrall paralyzyz etc.).

- in Kosovo their bomb damaged a 6 centuries old (and UNESCO protected) MONASTERY Gracanica - in Nis their bombs distroyed a HOSPITAL

- In Kragujevac they bombed the car industry (that producess Yugo) which feeds 35.000 families. As response to that workers have decided to form a 24h "wall of people" which would surround the factory and protect it with their and their families lives. they have sent the precise position of the factories both to NATO and media and a note saying that at least 1000 people will always be in or around the factory so if they want to bomb they will have to get ready to kill some people too.

- They have destroyed 30 SCHOOLS

- 40 OBJECTS WHICH ARE ALSO A RESIDENTIAL AREA

- They have hit a REFUGEE CAMP in Pristina and many civilians died!

- 30 people are already dead and more than 90 are wounded! and so on and on!

WHAT MILITARY OBJECTS ARE THESE? WHAT THREAT TO THE PEACE REPRESENT SCHOOLS, MONASTERIES, REFUGEE CAMPS? WHAT IS THAT GOING TO DO FOR THE WORLD PEACE?

You are my friends and I love you as if we were family and for that same reason I can't keep quite any more! THIS AGGRESSION AND THIS MASS MURDERS HAVE TO STOP! THIS MIGHT BE CALLED A "STEP TOWARD WORLD PEACE", BUT IT IS STILL A PLAIN MURDER!!!

PLEASE, STAND UP TO THAT AND HELP US PROTECT INOSCENT LIVES! DO NOT BELIEVE THAT THIS WILL BRING PEACE THIS WILL ONLY MAKE THINGS WORSE.

Just to prove this I will let you know, that before this all started no one wanted to go and fight in Kosovo, now there are so many volonteers that the Army doesn't have enough means to transport them all there! The troops are multiplying as we speak!!!

- Do not believe that by this you are preventing a humanitarian desaster! By this you are only making it!!!

- Do not believe that is a fair and unselfish act whose only motiv is of humanitarian nature! This is a big political game of interests! Of all the countries with humanitarian problems (Turkey, Ruanda etc.) Yugoslavia is the only one that was bombed!

- Do not believe that this will stop Milosevic, Kosovo is our cradle and this has united all the Serbs and made him even stronger! Therefore this bombings have destroyed any chance we ever had to get rid of him! Therefore you have sentenced us all to a slow and painful death!

PLEASE HELP US STOP THIS BEFORE ANY CHANCE FOR PEACE IN KOSOVO IS TOTALLY DESTROYED AND BEFORE WE GET HURT! PLEASE, HELP US STOP THIS BEFORE IT IS TOO LATE!

With faith in our friendship and in common sense and with love,

Tijana Mirovic

dieyetribe information collective

www.dieyetribe.com

"You are forwarding propaganda" - and my reply

March 30, 1999

Ken,

I was going to write you a long letter to try to explain to you that you are simply forwarding misguided propaganda, but you wouldn't believe the things that I've seen in the last several months in Kosovo (I was there as an aide worker). It upsets me that voices I expect to be reasonable are so easily misled.

Please take me off your list

Good luck in your other causes, but in this case you know not of what you write.

***

Dear subscriber,

Your one time presence in the country is hardly a qualification for calling eyewitness reports of civilian casualties and damage "misguided propaganda." How on earth would you know?

Yours is the exact claim made against the reporters who tried to report on the extensive civilian casualties in Iraq. Even the publisher of Harper's has written about the absolute censorship of news on civilian casualties in these attacks. The UN Iraq relief program director finally had to quit out of despair. There's nothing even original pointing these things out.

Do you deny the economic war against Nicaraguan civilians? Iraqi civilians? That the bombed Sudanese pharmaceutical plant was a pharmaceutical plant? Did you even read Michel Chossudovsky's article - written in 1996 - that precisely diagrammed the trajectory that has led us to where we are today?

No one denies atrocities in the region, but atrocities are hardly the reason for these NATO actions.

The US now admits to its role in the murder of 200,000 Guatemalans, nearly 20 years after the fact. Where were you on this? Calling the people who risked life and limb to report on this "misguided propagandists?"

The attack on Yugoslavia is part of a well established program of destroying the social and economic infrastructure of regions that threaten the "economic stability" of us and our closest economic partners. It's part and parcel of our "free" market. What do you think the military is for? Parades?

Cuba, Vietnam, Libya, Iraq, Nicaragua, even Italy right after WWII - any country with the means to demonstrate a viable alternative to the US economic order - is theatened, starved and/or bombed back into the stone age. There have been no exceptions. Do you think the banks, oil companies and industrial cartels that control the US news media and government would leave global economic development to chance, and thereby blithely put trillions of their dollars at risk? You are naive and uninformed if you do.

Yes, these countries are run by individuals who are "problematic," but if that were a qualification for a military invasion, we'd be bombing every capital on earth, including our own.

"Skeptical of civilian casualty accounts" - and my reply

March 31, 1999

Sorry to seem sceptical Ken, but unless you know this person or have some way of verifying who it is, I am. I'm watching the reports on the BBC, they are outright sceptical about the bombing and it's usefulness. They are specifically asking every refugee that leaves Kosovo "Are you leaving because of the bombing or because of the Serbs?" So far the answers have been 100% "because of the Serbs." The refugees seem to be behind NATO and their actions. The BBC has been criticized by the British government for their stance regarding the bombing. If indeed this post is from a personal friend, I'll take it all back, but in my opinion the Serbs are fighting a fairly dirty war on all fronts, including the Internet.

***

Thanks Bill. A number of people have, quite rightly, raised this point.

It's very possible there was a propagandistic element to the report. I should have prefaced the post with a disclaimer. Then again, I'd like to see such disclaimers posted on Pentagon, NATO, and IMF reports, too.

Anyway, the post was offered as an example of a voice most people are unlikely to hear. Clearly, I can't verify all the details. However, when one bombs populated areas, innocent people are often killed and injured and the US military/press corps has already demonstrated their ability to censor this news pretty much entirely no matter how gruesome it is (ex. Iraq, Panama, etc.).

That being said, I note that today's New York Times confirms *some* of what this individual posted to the Net several days ago: factories *were* targeted and the enmity between the two sides has been increased exponentially since the NATO bombing started.

Also, according to the Times, Belgrade and downtown government offices are going to become *official* targets. How do you bomb a downtown area without harming innocent people? "Smart bombs" that can do such things don't exist, regardless of what Pentagon press briefings say.

Rural Albanians no doubt fear the Serbs more than the aerial bombing, but that's not a recommendation for bombing Belgrade.

(Note 5/15/99: "The preceding paragraph is an example of our being taken in by NATO propaganda. We corrected this later by filing numerous reports from a variety of sources that demonstrate most Albanians and others fled to avoid being caught in the NATO war zone, not out of fear of "Serbs.")

The whole thing is an ugly mess, but according to at least one analyst, Michel Chossudovsky, who has been covering the Balkans for two decades, today's horrors were predictable ten years ago and the "democratic alliance" has done nothing but add fuel to the fire at every opportunity.

At the time of violent, unlawful interventions like these whether they are in Yugoslavia, Vietnam, Panama, Iraq,

Central America, or any one of dozens of other places, there is *always* a perfectly plausible cover story presented that seems to make our actions both necessary and morally correct.

Years later, when the truth ultimately comes out, the enormous human suffering created is shrugged off - if it is even acknowledged at all.

The Balkans have socialist leanings, educational and engineering sophistication, and oil under their ground. *Every* region with a similar profile, that is not in northern Europe, has been the subject of US violence (either overt or covert) for one reason or another. Can anyone believe this is a coincidence?

We can get caught up in the fireworks of the moment or we can ask "who is behind the scenes lighting the fuse?" The coincidence of every region that attempts a degree of economic independence from the "free" market, "spontaneously" self-combusting - one after another - leads me to reject the premise of the US/NATO invasion* and ask pointed and skeptical questions.

*It's illegal for US troops to engage in combat without a formal declaration of law. It would be nice to see that law enforced. But that too is not even a subject of discussion any more.

Former US state department official William Blum has written the textbook on US interventions around the world: "Killing Hope: US Military and CIA Interventions since World War II."

Instead of reading the latest propaganda from the latest blow up, step back and look at the pattern. It's quite unmistakable.

Consider the trillions of dollars the interlocked oil, arms, banking, and industrial cartels have at stake in an "orderly" pattern of global economic development. Is it plausible that these entities, which control the US news media and government, would choose to take a passive "live and let live" approach to who is allowed to develop and how?

Remember the $100,000,000 "chemical weapons" plant in Sudan we destroyed not too long ago? Even the NYT and the WashPost had to give up the effort of propping up that lie. That was the only indigenously owned pharmaceutical plant in the entire region. The suffering and economic consequences of that act of state sponsored terrorism was never even news, which speaks volumes about the "humanitarian" motives behind bombing the Balkans.

This action and others like it can be explained by one motivation: The "western democracies" are clearing the ground to make sure that their client states remain sources of cheap raw materials and markets for expensive finished goods.

It's the same reason the British Empire used violence to try to retain the American colonies. Nothing's changed except that our country has, disgracefully, become the one wielding the club.

Untangling intervention logic

March 31, 1999

DIALOG: UNTANGLING INTERVENTION LOGIC

Ken's Original Message:

We can get caught up in the fireworks of the moment or we can ask "who is behind the scenes lighting the fuse?" The coincidence of every region that attempts a degree of economic independence from the "free" market "spontaneously" self-combusting - one after another - leads me to reject the premise of the US/NATO invasion and ask pointed and skeptical questions.

*It's illegal for US troops to engage in combat without a formal declaration of law. It would be nice to see that law enforced. But that too is not even a subject of discussion any more.

Reader response:

You're sounding like a convservative (In the best meaning of the word).

Ken's Commentary:

I think one of the most successful applications of social engineering has been to split people along right/left lines when their interests and sensibilities are in reality nearly identical.

Who approves of tyranny and violations of the law? Who doesn't bristle at seeing innocent people being abused? Who wants his tax dollars wasted or used to inflict suffering in other parts of the world, or at home?

I'm sure we agree on many, many fundamental things, even if we have different views on the details. I guess I can best sum up my beliefs this way: I believe in the basic decency of the average person and the thorough indecency of the industrial system that's taken control of this country's government.

Reader response (continued):

I haven't researched it but I'm to understand that the NATO charter does not permit NATO to engage in offensive operations, only defensive ones.

Ken's Commentary:

There was quite a bit of activity on Albright's part last year negotiating the "modification" of these rules - well in advance, by the way, of the atrocities that supposedly triggered the invasion.

Reader response (continued):

It appears that those currently in power have no regard for the constitution, the rule of law, or in this case the NATO charter. It is quite sad as it marks our decline from civilization into barbarianism. Even sadder still is the lack of visible vocal opposition to our actions in Kosovo.

Ken's Commentary:

And I've received a good dose of hate mail for even *suggesting* that our motives are less than pure, from my Critical Mass list no less!

Reader response (continued):

Although I almost completely disagree with your logic and question the veracity of many of your factual assertions I find it interesting that we come to largely the same conclusions. I greatly appreciate your questioning and the legitimate questions that you raise.

Ken's Original Message:

...This action and others like it can be explained by one motivation: The "western democracies" are clearing the ground to make sure that their client states remain sources of cheap raw materials and markets for expensive finished goods.

Reader response (continued):

I don't know the thinking of those in power so I can't test your thesis, however, I would not be surprised to find that it is strongly held by some, and that they feel that they are protecting the US by destroying factories in the developing world that they do not control. I completely reject such notions.

Ken's Commentary:

I think that any decent person would.

I do have a little first hand experience with the people who populate the cutthroat world of "high" finance. When you consider the harm Wall Street intentionally inflicts on US citizens (who do you think sold the S & Ls all those garbage bonds in the 1980s, knowing full well they were crap?), imagine how much more ruthless the game is when the populations of other countries are concerned. There is not even the faintest bit of moral restraint - what most normal people feel as a matter of course - in these circles. Not a shred.

Reader response (continued):

We all lose when a factory or other institution is destroyed. The efforts of many are lost by such acts to all our detriment. I find it interesting that the war planners in WWII took pains to avoid historic and religious structures in our bombings of Europe.

Ken's Commentary:

And, supposedly, factories that were producing profits for Chase Manhattan (Standard Oil)-funded ventures were also spared. The method for the transfer of these profits, through "neutral" Switzerland, is only just *finally* being revealed. There was quite a bit of trading with the enemy going on before and even during the war. Some people were caught, tried, and convicted for this, including ex-president George Bush's father.

One of the only US journalists who took an interest in these stories was George Seldes. After the war, the issue went away fast and a heck of a lot of ex-Nazis found jobs with the US government, US industry (like Ford), and German reconstruction. Seldes was rewarded for these and similar journalistic efforts with, among other things, a dictate from the NYT publisher banning even the mention of his name from the pages of that paper.

(www.brasscheck.com/seldes)

I think careful study of the pre- and post-war support of German and Italian fascists by "big business" reveals much about the true allegiance of these entities. It's certainly not to democracy either, here or abroad. Crushing the economic and political aspirations of a small region of the world in order to guarantee a return on investment is certainly well within their capabilities and moral comfort zone.

(www.brasscheck.com/heartfield/rise.html)

Reader response (continued):

Not that we didn't destroy a few in any case. In Yugoslavia we seem to be specifically targeting such (cultural and religious) structures.

Ken's Commentary:

It makes it easier to put up McDonalds' in their place. Not that I believe this is the conscious plan, but clearly, if the cultural fabric is shredded sufficiently, it does make it that much easier for US commerce to move in during the "reconstruction" period.

About big business' control of the US government. I've yet to find a single federal agency that has not been totally co-opted by the corporations it was set up to regulate. And when there is draconian enforcement of federal regulations, it always falls on an individual or a small company, never one of the big boys.

A local example here in upstate NY: GE, in direct violation of court orders, permitted hundreds of gallons of PCPs to contaminate the Hudson River and has yet to be made to fix the problem. Yet if a family farm were to bulldoze a quarter acre wetlands or have a leaky diesel tank, the EPA or whoever regulates these things would have a SWAT team on their front porch (an admitted exaggeration, but you know what I mean).

As for big business being in charge of US foreign policy, which includes the use of the military, this has been documented pretty well in many cases. Interestingly, years after the fact, mainstream papers which normally operate as conduits for "free" market propaganda like the Times and the Washington Post have little trouble acknowledging these realities.

The best documented examples, I think, where big business worked consciously and hand in hand with the US government, were the coups in Chile (educated population, socialist tendencies, major mineral resources) and Guatemala (agrarian reform in a country owned by United Fruit).

In both cases, a particular company or group of companies' oxes were being gored and they simply used their influence to engage the CIA to organize a coup. In both cases, the president at the time (Eisenhower in Guat., Nixon in Chile) was easily persuaded to sign on, because they were "sold" on the idea that these countries were in danger of going communist.

Edward Bernays, the PR demon who convinced "modern" women that smoking cigarettes was a sign of liberation, helped broker the Guatemala deal using his long standing government connections. He was a graduate of the Creel Committee which sold the American public on our "need" to be involved in World War I, and United Fruit was one of his many post war clients. (Goebbels read Bernay's texts on propaganda, written explicitly to attract big business clients, and treasured them.)

Bernays conceived the communist scare story on the one hand and on the other hand arranged for junkets of American press people to visit Guatemala and enjoy the lavish hospitality of the United Fruit people. Meanwhile, the CIA coordinated a terror campaign on the ground.

With the US press blinded to the realities of the situation and the local military convinced they would be slaughtered if it didn't conform to US wishes, the democratically elected president of Guatemala was sent packing and our man was put in to preserve the status quo. The status quo being: independent subsistence farmers being removed from productive land at gunpoint and hired to work for poverty wages on foreign owned export plantations.

This is the same thing the British Empire did to the Irish 100+ years earlier with similar results: the destruction of independent, self-supporting communities; a steep decline in nutrition: man-made ecological disaster (potato famine in Ireland from the failure of a single crop, catastrophic landslides from a modest sized storm in Central America).

Nowhere is the military-government-banking coordination more clear cut than in export agribusiness. It's a little harder to dope out in places like the Balkans and Iraq.

(Few people know that pre-war Iraq was building its own fertilizer and pharmaceutical industries thereby denying US petrochemical firms the Iraqi market and challenging their markets in the Third World. Bush and Quayle family members, and their friends, were major shareholders of companies that were affected. A coincidence, I'm sure. As was the fact that the Bush State Department all but gave Hussein a personal invitation to invade Kuwait by explicitly stating that the Iraq-Kuwait border dispute - the Kuwaitis were stealing Iraqi oil with diagonal drilling technology - was a regional matter of no concern to the US. Since we put him in power, fed him, armed him and told him we didn't care about the dispute, delusional Saddam Hussein probably thought the invasion was no big deal. Thus started the biggest US military "adventure" since the Vietnam War. 1,000,000+ Iraqi CIVILIANS dead from sanctions, and counting.)

Note the Sudanese pharmaceutical plant that was leveled last year - also in violation of US law - without so much as an apology. It was the *only* indigenously owned plant of its type in the entire region. Has anyone explained that one yet? I think someone in intelligence with ties to the pharmaceutical industry figured they could slip that one in along with the Afghani raid and no one would notice or care. (The sad fact: he was right.)

Some commercial interest(s) - it could simply be the entities behind the IMF - have decided that the Balkans must not thrive without conforming to the "natural" order of things. Remember, today's conditions are nearly 20 years in the making. The bombing is only the most recent in a series of stages of this assault.

All this is theory, of course, which I agree I can't prove (today at least). But can anyone else come up with a better reason why we are - in direct violation of the rule of law and common sense - using our military there? It clearly has nothing to do with compassion, and the mere fact that Clinton & Co. are sociopaths is not an adequate explanation.

From Sam Smith - Balkan Stats

March 30, 1999

BALKAN NUMBERS & UNTANGLING INTERVENTION LOGIC

Some numbers on the Balkans that expose the sick absurdity of the "humanitarian" cover story:

From Sam Smith:

BALKAN STATS I

FROM A COLUMN BY TONY SNOW: Key members of the United States Senate sat slack-jawed through a confidential briefing last Thursday from the Clinton administration foreign-policy team. After the foreign-policy wise men asserted that the United States has a moral imperative to stop the murderous Serbian president, Slobodan Milosevic, one senator asked: How many Albanians have Milosevic's troops massacred this year? The president's emissaries turned ashen. They glanced at each other. They rifled through their papers. One hazarded a guess: "Two thousand?" No, the senator replied, that was the number for all of last year. He wanted figures for the last month - or even the year to date, since the president had painted such a grisly picture of genocide in his March 24 address to the nation. The senator pressed on. How often have such slaughters occurred? Nobody knew. As it turns out, Kosovo has been about as bloody this year as, say, Atlanta. You can measure the deaths not in the hundreds, but dozens. (I'm not trying to deny Milosevic's brutality here; only to provide some comparisons.) More people died last week in Borneo than have expired this year in Kosovar bloodshed - more died in a single Russian bomb blast; in a single outburst of violence in East Timor; in a single day in Rwanda. China has been bloodier this year.

BALKAN STATS II

--Estimated number of persons killed in Iraq due to American-led sanctions: over 1,000,000

--Estimated number of persons killed in the Sudan over the past 15 years: 1,500,000

--Estimated number of persons killed in Rwanda over the last five years: 500,000

--Estimated number of persons killed in Chechnya: 80,000

--Estimated number of people dying *each day* around the world because of lack of water, clothing, shelter, food or medicine: 100,000

--Estimated number of people in the world who go to bed hungry: 800,000,000

--Estimated number of persons killed in Kosovo last year: 2,000

BALKAN STATS III

--Estimate of new households watching CNN thanks to its war coverage: 472,000

BALKAN STATS IV

--Cost of America's 21 B-2 bombers: $42 billion

--Value of Yugoslavian GDP: $43 billion

***

Source of stats:

THE PROGRESSIVE REVIEW

Editor: Sam Smith

prorev.com

From Michel Chossudovsky - Recent Balkan history

March 31, 1999

* Recent Balkan History

- Multi-ethnic, socialist Yugoslavia was once a regional industrial power and economic success. In the two decades prior to 1980, annual GDP growth averaged 6.1 percent, medical care was free, the literacy rate was of the order of 91 percent, and the life expectancy was 72 years. But after a decade of Western economic ministrations and five years of disintegration, war, boycott, and embargo, the economies of the former Yugoslavia are prostrate, their industrial sectors dismantled.

- The Reagan administration targeted the Yugoslav economy in a "Secret Sensitive" 1984 National Security Decision Directive (NSDD 133), "United States Policy toward Yugoslavia." A censored version declassified in 1990 largely elaborated on NSDD 54 on Eastern Europe, issued in 1982. The latter advocated "expanded efforts to promote a 'quiet revolution' to overthrow Communist governments and parties" while reintegrating the countries of Eastern Europe into a market-oriented economy.

- IMF-sponsored programs since then continued the disintegration of the industrial sector and the piecemeal dismantling of the Yugoslav welfare state. Debt restructuring agreements increased foreign debt, and a mandated currency devaluation also hit hard at Yugoslavs' standard of living.

- In return for assistance, Yugoslavia agreed to even more sweeping economic reforms, including a new devalued currency, another wage freeze, sharp cuts in government spending, and the elimination of socially-owned, worker-managed companies.

- The reforms demanded by Belgrade's creditors struck at the heart of Yugoslavia's system of socially owned and worker-managed enterprises. As one observer noted, "The objective was to subject the Yugoslav economy to massive privatization and the dismantling of the public sector."

- Some Yugoslavs joined together in a doomed battle to prevent the destruction of their economy and polity. As one observer found, "worker resistance crossed ethnic lines, as Serbs, Croats, Bosnians and Slovenians mobilized... shoulder to shoulder with their fellow workers." But the economic struggle also heightened already tense relations among the republics -- and between the republics and Belgrade.

- While local leaders and Western interests share the spoils of the former Yugoslav economy, they have entrenched socio-ethnic divisions in the very structure of partition. This permanent fragmentation of Yugoslavia along ethnic lines serves to thwart a united resistance of Yugoslavs of all ethnic origins against the recolonization of their homeland.

- While rebuilding is sacrificed on the altar of debt repayment, Western governments and corporations show greater interest in gaining access to strategic natural resources... "Substantial" petroleum fields lie in the Serb-held part of Croatia just across the Sava river from Tuzla, the headquarters for the US military zone. Exploration operations went on during the war, but the World Bank and the multinationals which conducted the operations kept local governments in the dark, presumably to prevent them from acting to grab potentially valuable areas.

- Yugoslavia has been carefully erased from our collective understanding. Opinion-makers instead dogmatically present cultural, ethnic, and religious divisions as the sole cause of the crisis. In reality, they are the consequence of a much deeper process of economic and political fracturing.

- The consensus among donors and international agencies is that past macroeconomic reforms adopted under IMF advice had not quite met their goal and further shock therapy is required to restore "economic health" in Yugoslavia's successor states.

Source: Michel Chossudovsky (1996) Department of Economics, University of Ottawa excerpt from "Dismantling Yugoslavia, Colonizing Bosnia" from the book "The Globalization of Poverty"

***

On the historic kindness of international bankers...

"Except through a purgatory of misery and starvation, I cannot see how Ireland is to emerge into a state of anything approaching to quiet or prosperity."

- Charles Wood, chancellor of the exchequer during the Irish Famine.

Ireland was a net exporter of food during the famine that killed at least 1,000,000 people and displaced another 2,000,000 in a period of five years. British authorities actively discouraged relief efforts saying they were an encouragement to overpopulation.

April, 1999

April, 1999

In April, 1999, I went back to my regular work, because I was so naive as to believe that this illegal and immoral military assault could not continue much longer - and that, if it did, the news media (mainstream and alternative) would soon catch up with the efforts of an amateur journalist working part-time, and start covering the story properly.

By the end of April, it was clear this was not going to happen, so I resumed writing.

May, 1999

German government report: No genocide in Kosovo

May 4, 1999

"A lie can make it halfway around the world before truth has had a chance to put on its galoshes."

- Mark Twain

***

It appears the professional liars, and the mindless parrots who repeat their stories on TV, on the Internet and elsewhere, outdid themselves in this war.

Was there "genocide" in Kosovo? Not according to a year's worth of intelligence reports filed with German courts by the German Foreign Office.

Their latest opinion:

"Ethnic Albanians in Kosovo have neither been nor are now exposed to regional or countrywide group persecution in the Federal Republic of Yugoslavia."

Opinion of the Upper Administrative Court at Mÿnster, March 11, 1999 (Az: 13A3894/94.A).

Note the date. This assessment was produced by the German Foreign Office in response to a courts' request that was deciding the status of Kosovo-Albanian refugees in Germany. The new Luftwaffe started bombing with its American and British allies less than two weeks later.

Much, much more material showing that the German Affairs Office had studied and rejected the Kosovo genocide claim is available.

Original source (in German): Junge Welt

Passed along by Sam Smith:

prorev.com

Everything you need to know about Kosovo*

May 5, 1999

*But CNN was too busy showing you military briefings and automobile ads to tell you...

***

"White House officials... said the bombing of Yugoslavia would continue unabated until President Stobodan Milosevic had bent to allied demands."

- The New York Times, May 4, 1999

And what *exactly* are these demands - assuming that the German Foreign Office's March 11 assessment that there is no official persecution (let alone genocide) of Albanians in Kosovo is correct?

These are the demands Milosevic has refused:

7. NATO personnel shall be immune from any form of arrest, investigation, or detention by the authorities in the FRY (Federal Republic of Yugoslavia).

8. NATO personnel shall enjoy... free and unrestricted passage and unimpeded access throughout the FRY including associated airspace and territorial waters.

11. NATO is granted the use of airports, roads, rails and ports without payment...

15. [NATO shall have] the right to use all of the electromagnetic spectrum...

(Source: The Rambouillet Text of Feb. 23. Excerpts from Appendix (B))

In other words, in order to "bring peace" to the internal affairs of a sovereign country, NATO proposed a total military occupation of the entire Federal Republic of Yugoslavia. For refusing this, the country is being bombed back to the stone age.

And who are the "freedom fighters" fighting the "civil war" against the elected government of Yugoslavia that precipitated this catastrophe?

The Kosovo Liberation Army: 1) classified as a terrorist organization by the US State Department as recently as 1997, 2) reported to be a major player in the European heroin trade by Interpol, and 3) reputed by independent press to engage in acts of terror against civilians of all enthic backgrounds including Albanians.

As journalist Sam Smith points out, the KLA is a group that was illegal for US citizens to send contributions to not long ago. Now they're raising troops on US soil with the help of millions of dollars worth of free PR from the AP, the New York Times, and other equally braindead news outfits.

Let's see... drugs, terrorism, criminal membership, front page support from the AP, the New York Times and the DoD... couldn't be a CIA project, could it? Nah. The CIA has never organized and funded gangster insurgents with drug money and mainstream media support. Right? Just in Nicaragua, and Southeast Asia, and Afghanistan, and Bolivia, and...

By the way, Serbs, Gypsies, Serb Muslims, as well as ethnic Albanians have been made refugees by NATO's assault. Why do we ONLY hear about Albanian refugees? Tens of thousands of members of other ethhic groups have been made homeless and impoverished by NATO bombing in Yugoslavia as well. Why isn't that news?

War and the "Big Lie"

May 6, 1999

"It is a horrible irony that the very same people who believe they are defending an innocent group against persecution have instead been enrolled through the technique of the "Big Lie" to become cheerleaders to the moral successors of the Third Reich."

- Ken McCarthy

***

I have received more hate mail, more angry denunciations, more "take me off your list" for my reporting on Yugoslavia than any single subject I've covered. This is very odd because nearly all the things I've reported that have engendered such a response have eventually ended up front page news - a month or so later.

Here is a polite excerpt of a typical angry response I received today:

"I'm surprised that you would suggest the genocide of Albanians by the Serbs is some kind of manufactured lie."

First, I've never suggested that. I've only reported what the German Foreign Affairs Office (equivalent to our State Department) said on the matter before the NATO assault began.

Here it is for anyone who missed it:

"Ethnic Albanians in Kosovo have neither been nor are now exposed to regional or countrywide group persecution in the Federal Republic of Yugoslavia." (Thesis 1)

Opinion of the Upper Administrative Court at Mÿnster, March 11, 1999 (Az: 13A 3894/94.A).

Second, I have pointed out that the evidence of deliberate state sponsored genocide in Yugoslavia that has been presented to the public so far has been flimsy at best. The report of a New York Times reporter of what a NATO spokesman says someone else reported to him, who received his information from someone else, who says he got it directly from someone who spoke to an eye witness, is not evidence. God help all of us if it is.

There is a segment of the population that has, like Pavlov's dogs, heard the word "genocide" and swallowed NATO disinformation campaign whole and become cheerleaders for the bombing and the impending ground war. Haven't these people ever heard of the "Big Lie?"

"The size of the lie is a definite factor in causing it to be believed, for the vast masses of the nation are in the depths of their hearts more easily deceived than they are consciously or intentionally bad. The primitive simplicity of their minds renders them a more easy prey to the big lie than a small one, for they themselves often tell little lies but would be ashamed to tell a big one."

"Never mind whether it is plausible or not. The victor will not be asked, later on, whether he told the truth or not. It is not Right that matters but Victory. Have no pity. Adopt a brutal attitude... Right is on the side of the strongest."

These are the statements of Adolph Hitler. He was not the first to use the "Big Lie" as a justification for naked aggression - nor was he the last as NATO's obscene assault on Yugoslavia demonstrates on a daily basis.

News media lies prolong the suffering of the innocent. The first victims of war are always children and the elderly and others least able to defend themselves. The death toll of our last "adventure" (in Iraq which is ongoing, new bombs dropped last night) is estimated to be as high as 1,000,000 civilian casualties as the result of contaminated water, starvation, and lack of medical care.

***

Here is a letter I have taken to sending to every newspaper that continues to parrot the NATO/White House line that the Albanians have suffered genocide at the hands of the Yugoslavian government. If you agree with my sentiments, you might send something similar.

May 6, 1999

Dear Editor:

The Third Reich and the holocaust it was responsible for was made possible in large part by the European and US news media. Through a combination of sloth, venality, and cowardice, it failed to report facts that were available to anyone who cared to look.

It is for this reason that I implore you to stop repeating the claims of NATO and the Pentagon against the Yugoslavian government, and therefore its people, until you have personally reviewed the evidence.

Only one credible organization, the German Foreign Office (the equivalent of our State Department), has studied the situation in Kosovo and published its results. Their conclusion:

"Ethnic Albanians in Kosovo have neither been nor are now exposed to regional or countrywide group persecution in the Federal Republic of Yugoslavia." (Thesis 1)

Opinion of the Upper Administrative Court at Mÿnster, March 11, 1999 (Az: 13A 3894/94.A)

The study was requested by a German Court involved in deciding immigration policy. Note the date of the conclusion.

Another German court, reviewing the results of earlier research, came to this conclusion:

"The Foreign Office's status reports of May 6, June 8 and July 13, 1998, given to the plaintiffs in the summons to a verbal deliberation, do not allow the conclusion that there is group persecution of ethnic Albanians from Kosovo. Not even regional group persecution, applied to all ethnic Albanians from a specific part of Kosovo, can be observed with sufficient certainty. The violent actions of the Yugoslav military and police since February 1998 were aimed at separatist activities and are no proof of a persecution of the whole Albanian ethnic group in Kosovo or in a part of it. What was involved in the Yugoslav violent actions and excesses since February 1998 was a selective forcible action against the military underground movement (especially the KLA) and people in immediate contact with it in its areas of operation... A state program or persecution aimed at the whole ethnic group of Albanians exists neither now nor earlier."

IV: Opinion of the Bavarian Administrative Court, October 29, 1998 (Az: 22 BA 94.34252):

It is a horrible irony that the very same people who believe they are defending an innocent group against persecution have instead been enrolled through the technique of the "Big Lie" to become cheerleaders to moral successors of the Third Reich.

You now have in your hands a credible report that contradicts the very serious and inflammatory claims against Yugoslavia that appear on your editorial pages. What are you going to do about it?

Your bombing bill

May 6, 1999

By the way, guess who's paying for the bombing of Yugoslavia?

***

SEND THIS MESSAGE FAR AND WIDE; LET'S FLOOD THOSE PHONE LINES TO CONGRESS

From: Darien De Lu

Subject: Call Congress - Oppose War Funds

IMMEDIATE ACTION ALERT:

The Kosovo Supplemental Appropriations Bills will be voted on by both the House and the Senate this week or early next week. The House vote is scheduled for tomorrow Thursday, May 6th.

The House Appropriations Committee added $6.8 billion to the President's $6 billion request before sending it to the floor. They have used the bill to load in the increased spending that was going to violate the FY2000 defense budget caps. Their intention is to free up the later appropriations bill for more outrageous pork. The Pentagon doesn't need any more money whatsoever.

For more information about the House bill, see analysis below.

Call your Representative at 202-225-3121 or

Senators at 202-224-3121

Do it today to let them know you oppose the emergency spending bill and increased military spending for any purpose and urge them to vote against the supplemental appropriations bills except for emergency aid for refugees from Kosovo.

To get all your elected officials' contact information and voting records, go to the Vote Smart webpage, or call Project Vote-Smart free at 1-888-868-3762.

Gillian

***

Kosovo Supplemental Appropriations Bill: Republicans Load Up the Bill for a War Most Oppose; Layaways for Pork in Fiscal 2000

On Thursday, April 29, the House Appropriations Committee voted for a $12.9 billion Kosovo "emergency" supplemental appropriations bill, more than double the Administration request for $6 billion to pay for the war in Kosovo.

The Committee majority resorted to a shell game to avoid charges of adding pork to the bill to pay for a war. They loaded programs into the supplemental appropriations bill that have nothing to do with the war in order to clear room for pork requests in the fiscal 2000 Defense Appropriations bill.

As Rep. David Obey (D-WI), ranking Democrat on the House Appropriations Committee pointed out yesterday: "I do not believe that we should be using something as serious as the war in order to simply make a lot of headroom for somebody's pork that will be added in the defense bill down the line."

Three important points to note in the $6.9 billion hike in military spending:

1. The extra money approved by the House Appropriations Committee will come out of social security surpluses. Less than two weeks after Congress passed the fiscal 2000 budget resolution in which Members of both parties pledged to protect social security, the House Republican majority has now countenanced a $6.9 billion raid out of a program that just days before they argued must be protected by a "lock box."

2. Republicans who denounce President Clinton for neglecting military needs should stand accused of similar neglect. In October 1998, six months ago, the Republicans leadership had an opportunity to pay for essential programs that the President had supposedly shortchanged. Instead they pumped money into other pet projects. After President Clinton requested $1.1 billion to deal with readiness problems last fall, Congress appropriated $8.3 billion in the October emergency supplemental bill -- but managed to neglect the shortfalls that they now find so critical. Between 1995 and 1998 the Republican Congress added $23 billion to defense budget requests; only 10% of the money added went to the O&M and personnel accounts.

3. Much of the so-called emergency funding is motivated by Republicans' desire to spend money in fiscal 1999 that does not count against the fiscal 2000 budget caps to free funding for pork projects in fiscal 2000.

Rep. Obey accurately described the decisions of the House Appropriations Committee: "I find it mind- boggling that some of the same members who yesterday voted against the operation will today vote to more than double the amount of spending that the president has asked for to conduct those operations."

[Excerpted from analysis by John Isaacs, Council for a Livable World]

Gillian Gilhool

Legislative Organizer

WILPF

www.wilpf.org

The War and Social Security

May 6, 1999

PAYING FOR THE DESTRUCTION OF ONE SOCIETY BY LOOTING THE RETIREMENT SAVINGS OF ANOTHER

Students of propaganda and the US news media (is there a difference?) cannot have failed to notice the steady drumbeat over the past few years calling for the privatization of Social Security.

The plan? Move the fund from its stable, extremely low overhead management to the abler, more dynamic hands of Wall Street money managers.

In order to make this act of madness more palatable, we've been told, incessantly, that Social Security is running out of money (lie #1) and the fund is badly managed (lie #2). The management of the fund is accomplished at a cost that is a tiny fraction of what any of the privatization schemes promise, and as many starry-eyed mutual fund players should have learned by now, fund management is not free, far from it, especially the way Wall Street cuts the cards.

As several people pointed out to me, the $6.9 billion hike in military spending ADDED to the $ 6 billion the commander-in-sleeze asked for to continue bombing the people of Yugoslavia is coming from... the US Social Security surplus. And the US news media is silent.

I thought I'd seen everything.

Running working state managed institutions into the ground and then crying that they need to be "privatized" is an old game, but never have the stakes been higher. The amount of public money that will disappear when Social Security is put under the "stewardship" of Wall Street will make the S&L scandal look restrained in comparison.

And this war, this immoral, illegal, abominable war is being used as a smokescreen to move this financial disaster one more step closer to reality.

And whose money is it that created the Social Security surplus that is now going to be used for bombs? Filmmaker Rick Goldsmith "Tell the Truth and Run"

www.brasscheck.com/seldes fills us in:

About that Social Security surplus:

Social Security taxes comes from working men and women and families.

The burger flipper making $6/hour pays 6.2% of his income to Social Security to pay for the bombing. The factory worker making $350/week pays 6.2% of her income to Social Security to pay for the bombing.

The teacher making $30,000/year pays 6.2% of her income to Social Security to pay for the bombing.

The tax accountant making $200,000/year pays 2% of his earned income to Social Security to pay for the bombing. The CEO (of that munitions factory that makes a bundle from the war) making $1,000,000/year pays less than 1/2 of 1 percent of his salary to Social Security to pay for the bombing.

The heir to the family fortune (of that weapons manufacturer that makes a bundle from the war), who lives on the Wall Street-invested interest to that fortune, pays nothing to Social Security to pay for the bombing.

I don't know about you, but I plan to be in Washington DC June 5th.

Enough is enough.

Radioactive rounds finally acknowledged by US press

May 7, 1999

1. Radioactive rounds finally acknowledged by mainstream press

2. The origins of the Serb genocide charge

3. The American Legion - bashers of war protesters for nearly 80 years - comes out AGAINST the war

4. 100,000++ invisible refugees

5. Memories of cluster bombs

***

1. The San Francisco Examiner finally reported today that NATO is using radioactive (so-called "depleted" uranium) rounds in Yugoslavia. We first posted this information on April 8 and it was already old news then.

Source: *International Action Center

www.iacenter.org

2. We first posted this on March 24 about the roots of the genocide charge - might be worth reviewing. It was for me. Know your sources.

What we aren't hearing in the U.S. media

Military expansion in the Balkans is being justified by reports of an alleged massacre of Albanians in Kosovo. The reports are based on accusations made by William Walker from the U.S. State Department. Walker heads the Kosovo Verification Mission. But Walker's account has been strongly disputed by several major European newspapers, including Le Monde and Le Figaro. These papers assert that the allegations of a massacre are a fabrication.

Walker is not an independent, neutral observer. He represents the U.S. government. He has a sordid history in his years of work in Central America with U.S.-trained death squads in El Salvador. And he was responsible for setting up a so-called humanitarian operation that was used as a cover for the Contra war to overthrow the government of Nicaragua.

Source: *International Action Center

www.iacenter.org

3. Some astonishing news about an unprecedented event sent along by Stan Smith. The American Legion leadership has voted unanimously to call for a complete withdrawal of all US military from Yugoslavia.

"We believe the best thing we can do to support our troops, to protect our troops, is to bring them home," said Harold L. "Butch" Miller, national commander of major veterans organization.

"We believe we are getting into a bad situation in Kosovo." The Legion's national executive committee unanimously adopted a resolution Wednesday calling for all U.S. soldiers, pilots and support staff to be removed from the region. The statement said the NATO attacks "could only lead to troops being killed, wounded or captured without advancing any clear purpose, mission or objective."

For those who puzzle over the American Legion Halls that dominate small town America (there's an active one a two minute walk from my home), the Legion was founded in 1919 after World War I as a veteran's mutual support group, but immediately took on an aggressive "anti-Bolshevik" stance.

The founders originally considered becoming an armed paramilitary force to help suppress dissent, and pioneer members organized raids in many cities, burned literature, confisticated membership lists and had the leaders of many "radical" groups arrested.* Ultimately, the Legion settled into the more low key role of an unarmed volunteer intelligence and propaganda auxiliary for the military. Part of their function has been to wave the flag for every US military operation, good, bad or indifferent.

That the Legion has refused to salute this war is a first and an encouraging sign that common sense, if not decency, is asserting itself in spite of the Pentagon-CNN barrage.

This must be the first time that the American Legion and the International Action Center have agreed on anything.

* Army Surveillance in America, 1775-1980. Jensen, Joan. Yale University Press, 1991.

4. Note that when scenes of refugee camps are shown, no one mentions the fact that there are also tens of thousands of Gypsies, Serb Muslims, Serb Christians, and other minorities who have been made homeless since the NATO bombing started. That should signal the astute that something in the reporting is fundamentally amiss and the propaganda element is high.

5. Here's a statement from Tom Hayden who has seen this all before (thanks to SF's tenacious citizen guardian Doug Comstock for sending this along):

LOS ANGELES TIMES -- Wednesday, May 5, 1999

AS THE INNOCENT DIE, WHERE ARE ALL THE VOICES OF PROTEST?

Balkans: The liberals' silence on the NATO bombing and its 'collateral damage' is keeping us from talking about alternatives.

By TOM HAYDEN

Where are the voices of protest against the suffering inflicted on civilians and children by our bombardment of Serbia?

The moral rationale provided by the Clinton administration at the outset of the bombing was that the brutal ethnic cleansing of Kosovo could be stopped in a short military campaign. That promise was either a deception or a delusion. The war has turned into a horrific quagmire, and yet even liberal Democrats remain strangely tongue-tied about the suffering, which our government lamely calls "collateral damage."

Every day seems to bring news of civilians being killed and the White House apologizing. Worse, according to the Wall Street Journal, President Clinton and British Prime Minister Tony Blair pushed in mid-April for a wider definition of targets that would increase the danger to civilians. The result is the death of cleaning ladies and bus drivers, evacuation of 85,000 people from Belgrade neighborhoods poisoned by toxic chemicals, the unemployment of 100,000 Serbs and laying waste of Serbia's civilian infrastructure with what the New York Times calls "greater effects on the gross domestic product than the Nazi and, then, the Allied bombing of Yugoslavia" during World War II. And the silence continues. Perhaps the silent ones think these are all regrettable accidents, or that war is hell, or that bombing Serb civilians who have opposed Milosovic in the past will help them to overthrow him now. What then of the intentional indiscriminate infliction of shrapnel wounds on children? Unexploded cluster bomb units are turning whole areas of Yugoslavia into a "no man's land," wounding large numbers of children in the process. According to the Los Angeles Times, the director of Pristina's hospital says he has never done so many amputations as he has since victims of the weapon started coming in.

I keep an early model of the cluster bombs used in Vietnam on my shelf as a reminder of the evil done in the name of good intentions. The bombs are dropped over a broad landscape, where they explode via timers or the simple vibration of a passerby. The blast causes up to 300 pieces of deadly shrapnel to scatter in all directions. The shrapnel is very difficult to remove because of its deliberately jagged design.

Liberal silence on these issues allows Pentagon and NATO spokesmen to systematically and routinely utilize doublespeak and refuse to discuss the kinds of weapons they are using.

There seem to be two reasons for the Democratic war fever.

First, invocation of the Holocaust analogy has led many to accept Ted Koppel's admonition to "get used to the idea of civilian casualties." But is this the Holocaust or is it intervention in a long-standing Balkan religious and ethnic war? Whatever the answer, is there no level of civilian suffering that makes the bombing unjustifiable? And most important, isn't the U.S. and NATO military commitment to stop ethnic cleansing in the Balkans even slightly suspicious given the ethnic cleansing that they tolerate in Tibet, Turkey, Guatemala, Rwanda and Angola? Is this war really about human rights or about consolidating the U.S. and NATO as an alternative to the United Nations?

Second, the fact that President Clinton and his European social democratic allies started the bombing leads a majority of Democrats to rally behind their party leader. This was acceptable when the issue was belittling the president's sexual indiscretions to avoid impeachment, but it is quite something else to become apologists for the killing of children with anti-personnel bombs to shore up Western "credibility."

The Democratic Party's domestic agenda will be unraveled by the new liberal militarism. Already the Republican Congress has forced Clinton to accept $13 billion in military funds, twice what the president requested. By contrast, the president will ask for just $1 billion this year for new teachers and $5 billion over five years for school overcrowding.

I want to continue deepening and expanding the president's domestic agenda of investing in schools and jobs in the inner city, providing health care and restoring the natural environment.

Three decades ago, I was pursuing the same agenda when the Democratic Party started the Vietnam War and abandoned its commitment to a great society. That experience should not be repeated.

Before this becomes a Vietnam in the Balkans, it is time for liberals to start breaking their silence. The Jesse Jackson mission, opposed by the White House, plainly proves that diplomatic alternatives, like a partitioned Kosovo under the U.N., have not been exhausted.

Instead, the much-touted Apache gunships with American crews are preparing to escalate the conflict. The real Apaches, the Native Americans, were victims of a brutal, even genocidal, ethnic cleansing by the U.S. armed forces in the last century. That our government can self-righteously go to war to save Kosovo with helicopters named after the victims of our own ethnic cleansing measures the state of denial we are in.

***

Tom Hayden is a Democrat representing parts of West Los Angeles and the San Fernando Valley in the State Senate - and one of the few decent people left in California politics.

On the accuracy of bombing

May 8, 1999

FACTS:

75% of all dumb bombs in Desert Storm landed off target

93% of all bombs dropped in Desert Storm were conventional ("dumb")

Source: US Air Force (after the war was over)

***

The latest NATO massacres:

* It's easier to get information about China's *protests* than to get details about the destruction of their embassy in Belgrade by NATO missles yesterday (Source: Yahoo Asia)

* NATO drops cluster bombs on marketplace, hospital (Source: Yahoo Asia)

"I survived World War II, but I haven't seen anything like this," Mrs. Smilja Djuric, 73

* An incomplete list of NATO bombs and missles that have killed civilians (refered to by the military industrial-media complex as "blunders.") (Source: Yahoo Asia)

* All about cluster bombs

"The bomblet case is made of scored steel designed to break into approximately 300 preformed ingrain fragments (heavy shrapnel) for defeating light armor and personnel. 202 of these bomblets are loaded in each dispenser enabling a single payload attack against a variety and wide area coverage."

202 "bomblets" times 300 fragments = 60,600 shrapnel fragments per payload. Many bomblets sit in the ground unexploded, detonating later when disturbed.

During Desert Storm (alone) the US Air Force dropped 10,035 CBU-87s, a variety of cluster bomb.

Cost per "bomblet" = $13,941

Cost of one payload = $2,816,082

Manufacturer: Aerojet General / Honeywell

* NATO is using cluster bombs at this point because they're close to exhausting other munitions options. Wars are often about little more than liquidating inventory so that arms merchants can have a new selling season. You'll never guess where the US military stashed billions of dollars worth of equipment and arms intended for but never used in the Pacific Theater right after World War II: South Korea and South Vietnam. Foresight? Coincidence? "Luck"?

A review:

April 13, 1999

- On the accuracy of bombing

"After the war was over, the Air Force announced that laser- and radar- guided bombs made up just 7% of all U.S.

explosives dropped on Kuwait and Iraq. The other 93% were conventional "dumb" bombs, dropped primarily by high flying B-52s from the Vietnam era.

Ten percent of those "smart" bombs missed their targets, the Air Force said, while ***75% of the dumb bombs were off target.*** In all, about 62,000 tons - or 70% - missed their targets."

Source: John McArthur, "Second Front: Censorship and Propaganda in the Gulf War" p. 161

***

All told, one hundred and twenty MILLION pounds of high explosives "missed" their intended targets during Desert Storm. These are the Air Force's own figures. How can they be surprised by civilian casualties?

Recall that not long ago, these "blunders" were written off as "Serb propaganda."

Concerning China

May 9, 1999

"We only ask that enough people know what happened here and how it happened and why it happened, and that they work hard to see that it never happens anywhere again."

- Shinzo Hamai, Mayor of Hiroshima

***

Missing from today's headlines is reference to the fact that due to security lapses of incomprehensible incompetence by America's "intelligence community," China has in recent years acquired some of the US's most vital secrets regarding its nuclear offense technology and has enough information to be able to duplicate key parts of it.

And now, in the process of prosecuting a war, seemingly on behalf of a drug dealing, CIA supported, terrorist group, the KLA, we have accidentally bombed the Chinese embassy in Belgrade because...

The CIA told the military that the embassy, a well known, long established facility in downtown Belgrade, was an ammunitions depot.

(By the way, thanks to this lapse, we now know, for the first time, who's been providing NATO with its extensive and detailed list of targets for this assault.)

As John Stockwell's book by the same name puts it so well, the people who control US foreign policy - the same secret government that conducted the illegal war in Central America and created the conditions for the US war in Vietnam - are perpetually "in search of enemies."

***

"In order to bring a nation to support the burdens of maintaining great military establishments, it is necessary to create an emotional state akin to war psychology. There must be the portrayal of an external menace. This involves the development to a high degree of the nation-hero, nation-villain ideology and the arousing of the population to a sense of sacrifice. Once these exist, we have gone a long way on the path to war."

- John Foster Dulles

Who profits from war? The military contractors who make the weapons, the super wealthy who lend to governments by buying their bonds so they can carry on their wars, and the press which, in effect, profits by selling tickets to the show. Then there are all those who benefit from the country becoming more regimented and alienated from its own highest principles.

Ted Turner's recent hysteric declaration that we are on the verge of nuclear war is as transparent a demonstration of how all this works as there can be. For years now, CNN has promoted US "intervention" around the world and has contributed mightily towards making sure that Americans are confused and misled as to the nature of the assault on Yugoslavia. Now, in an appalling act of self-serving recklessness, Turner seeks to boost CNN's ratings even further. (And the Washington

Post did its bit by making sure his "fuel on the fire" analysis received the widest possible audience.)

Knowledge of how wars are started used to be widespread amongst educated, literate people before WWII. After the First World War books like "Merchants of Death" and "The Private Manufacture of Arms" were best sellers and one author who documented the process, Philip Noel-Baker, won a Nobel Prize for his efforts. The latter book is now so scarce, it can't be found on Bibliofind *or* Advanced Book Exchange.

"We are in the hands of an organization of crooks. They are the generals, politicians, manufacturers of armaments and journalists. All of them are anxious for unlimited expenditure, and go on inventing wars to terrify the public and to terrify the Ministers of the Crown."

- Lord Welby, Britain's principal Permanent Secretary to the Treasury, quoted in "The Private Manufacture of Arms."

Today, this once clear sighted, common sense knowledge of the workings and pathology of power is submerged in a deep media and academia-induced amnesia.

***

Concerning the present dilemma with China, there is no way the Chinese will ever believe the bombing of their embassy was a mistake and the government there is reacting accordingly. Little more than a week ago, an entirely peaceful and politically well connected group received a stern national rebuke for conducting a quiet and orderly civil rights protest in Beijing. Now the Chinese media and government (*obviously* the same thing in China) are openly encouraging what is, in effect, the taking of the staff of the American Embassy in Beijing hostage.

It is not inconceivable that China will send troops to Yugoslavia in order to protect its remaining citizens there. They've amply demonstrated that a military action would pose no internal problems for them and indeed, there are in China the very same elements as there are here who would stand to gain much from such a move.

"News shocks" have a way of making people forget everything that preceded them. It's important to keep in mind as we go through level after level of escalation, that this is all being manufactured. There is nothing accidental - or inevitable - about any of it.

The group that helped create the conditions for the war, and created the cover of lies to "sell" it, is the very same group that left the door open to our military secrets and directed the know-nothing military to bomb the Chinese embassy.

There is a cure for the present crisis. Stop the bombing and expose the currently nameless, faceless individuals who put the Chinese embassy on Nato's "hit" list and disclose how it happened. (While they're at it perhaps they can also explain how the CIA came to tell the US military and the commander in-sleeze that a $100,000,000 pharmaceutical plant in Sudan was a chemical weapons lab.)

Watch carefully. This simple common sense solution will not even be proposed.

Think about it: An organization that answers to no one can bring us to the brink, but its operations are so protected, so above any law, that we can't even expect to be given the name of the person or persons who made the supposed "mistake" or any information as to how such an inconceivable blunder could have been made.

And, of course, the media isn't probing too hard. Instead, they'll run inflammatory footage of anti-US riots and offer speculations on the future of US-China relations. Apparently this pseudo information is the best we're going to get as we try to make sense of the latest US-created madness from Yugoslavia.

"... the body bags have arrived"

May 10, 1999

"If a person wanted to start World War III based on the model that took place for World War I, you would do exactly what we are doing. You would go in there and say to Russia and China, we don't care what you say, we are going to get involved in a war here and rub their nose in it. Keep in mind that China and Russia have missiles that will reach the United States of America and they have every different kind of weapon of mass destruction to put on those missiles."

Statement made on April 29, 1999 (source at end of this post).

Meanwhile, I've been trying to find a mainstream, or alternative, news media account that will answer two simple questions:

1) How long was the Chinese Embassy at its present location and

2) How far *exactly* was it from the ammunitions depot it was supposedly mistaken for. All I've heard is "several hundred yards." Several football field lengths.

I got the answer to first question from 74 year old Ivanka Besevi in Belgrade:

"...The building was built in 1992, especially for the Chinese. The builders even used Chinese architectural plans. It was beautiful. It was never anything else but the Chinese Embassy.

It's... hard to believe that the American press is quite so gullible... Why didn't they simply buy a current map in any store, in any country of Europe? It couldn't have cost more than a dollar. A joke, that story."

"German Spiegel magazine reported that from sanctions previous to the war, our economy has been brought down to the 1968 level, and that the war has pushed it further, to the 1948 level... The military has not been hurt - they are fast, in small units, well organized and of low profile. A blundering giant is easy to avoid, if you are not a civilian. It is our factories, neighborhoods, bridges, TV stations, schools and our own broken bodies that are the most successful targets."

Source: Ivanka Besevi, May 10th edition of www.keepfaith.com

Also, it appears that some of the "refugee camps" in Albania are not what they appear to be which may explain why the refugee numbers have been so grossly inflated:

"...we were approaching 400 sorties (per day) coming out of Ramstein Air Force Base. These are C-17's (troop air transport) carrying our equipment into Albania. You go over there and get on the ground (and) all (the) troops are in tent cities, you see everything over there is American."

I'll reveal my source for this information later. First, here's what else this eye witness observer has to say:

"I interviewed some of these refugees two days ago. When I interviewed the refugees, I found some things to be tremendously interesting. They all said the same thing: In fact, they didn't have any problems until the bombing started.

"...the President is breaking the law today. I was over there just the last three days and I went in there aboard a C-17. That C-17 had multiple launch rockets, all of them hot, ready to be fired, two of those, along with two pallets of additional ammunition, a humvee, and a bunch of troops. So troops are over there right now, within sight of the border of Kosovo."

"...one of the units that got in there when I got there was the mortician unit. So the body bags have arrived."

Source: United States Senator James M. Inhofe Chairman of the Senate Armed Services Readiness Subcommittee April 29, 1999 - Delivered from the floor of the Senate

Note the date.

Did you know a US Senator was saying these things from the floor of the Senate just ten days ago?

But Senator Joseph Biden did get a chance to have *his* voice heard. This Sunday on "Meet the Press" he said:

"...but the Europeans have never led anything. We are a European power. If we are not pushing this, the whole thing will collapse."

That message was brought to you courtesy of General Electric (NBC) (www.brasscheck.com/nukenews.html) which is also, along with ABC, CBS, and CNN, making sure you don't hear what Senator Inhofe has to say.

Could the situation and the forces that are pushing forward be any clearer?

Compassion for the refugees

May 11, 1999

Two stories about the compassion for ethnic Albanians shown by NATO...

Story one:

CAMPAIGN LAUNCHED IN NORTHERN ALBANIA FOR REFUGEE RELOCATION

KUKES, Albania, May 11 (AFP) - An information campaign was launched Tuesday among the Kosovar refugees in the northern Kukes area of Albania in a bid to convince them to relocate to other areas because of threats to their security.

Most refugees reacted poorly to the campaign with some even showing open hostility to the idea of being moved.

Workers from the United Nations High Commissioner for Refugees (UNHCR) and local authorities arrived first at a camp run by Medecins Sans Frontieres and a site housing dozens of tractors brought by refugees from Kosovo.

Posters were put up around the MSF camp on Tuesday as UNHCR workers with megaphones read out the contents.

The refugees were told to leave Kukes because of its proximity to Serb artillery across the border. They were also told that the area was too small to cope with so many refugees and that more aid was available elsewhere.

A small group gathered around a representative of the Kukes municipality, but remained skeptical of the proposed relocation.

They said they did not want to travel "two days and two nights" with their tractors, which they refused to leave behind, and that in any case they had no fear of the Serb cannons.

They also said that they did not know how the sick, the old and the handicapped could be moved and that they wanted to stay as close to Kosovo as possible in case they could return home.

Women refugees said they did not want to leave because they were still waiting for their husbands and sons, who had stayed behind in the troubled province.

Discussions broke down when the impatient government official told the refugees that if they did not like the proposal they could go back to Kosovo.

"We want people to understand that these camps are temporary... We're not going to abandon these people but we're going to make it a little less comfortable for them to stay," (UNHCR spokeswoman Melita Sunjic) said.

Source: AFP-Agence France Presse

***

Story two:

KOSOVO REFUGEES TO MOVE TO ALBANIA

In Geneva, a spokeswoman today said the United Nations is running out of money for Kosovo refugees. UNHCR has received only $71 million of the $143 million it said it needed for its Kosovo operations.

"It has all been spent or fully committed," spokeswoman Judith Kumin said. "If there are no new contributions, it means that we're not able to continue to procure relief supplies which the refugees need."

In Kukes, on the Albanian border with Kosovo, the UNHCR began tent-to-tent lobbying to try to persuade refugees to move further into the country and out of range of Serb artillery.

"It's going to be very difficult. These people have been here a while, they're giving us very good, cogent reasons why they shouldn't leave," said spokesman Ray Wilkinson. "It's going to be a hard sell."

Source: Associated Press

ANALYSIS: If there are 1.5 million refugees, then $143 million works out to $9.53 US per refugee *if* the $72 million dollar shortfall is collected. Assuming an optimistic 100 days of displacement, that's about 10 cents per day for people who left their homes with whatever they could load into their tractor drawn wagons.

For comparison, one payload of cluster bombs costs over $2 million (not including delivery charges). Thirty five runs (a day's bombing?) equals the total amount received for refugee relief so far.

***

Note: 5/17/99 NATO is running in excess of five hundred bombing missions per day.

***

If there are no resources available to feed the refugees, why move them deeper into Albania and further away from their homes and land? Many of the displaced are subsistence farmers who are perfectly capable of feeding themselves which is why they are unwilling to be parted from or move their tractors further from home. There's still time to put a crop in the ground though a lot of precious time has been lost.

Note how the UN needs to propagandize to inspire the refugees to fear Serb artillery attacks. As US Senator James M. Inhofe, Chairman of the Senate Armed Services Readiness Subcommittee, said from the floor of the Senate over a week ago, the refugees are afraid of only one thing: NATO.

So NATO has driven these people off their land, caged them in poorly funded refugee camps, and is, with the help of the UN, actively discouraging them from returning home.

And why does NATO need the real estate in Northern Albania freed up? As Senator Inhofe pointed out, we may not be able to fly in relief supplies, but the US military has been working overtime creating and equipping a staging area for a ground invasion.

Where are all the people who were so worked up about unverified, and, in some cases, obviously falsified charges, of "genocide" now?

Stress, poor nutrition, inadequate sanitation, and disease can kill more quickly and in greater numbers than any military machine, especially among the infirm, the frail elderly, and infants.

The UN goes to market

May 11, 1999

"...the answer lies not in pouring more soldiers into the jungle, but rests in the hearts and minds of the... people."

- General Sir Gerald Templar, the High Commissioner of the British-occupied Federation of Malaya (1952) originator of "civic action" as a branch of warfare whose tactics served as a model for the United States in Vietnam.

***

Today I was puzzling over the bizarre role the UN is playing in the NATO-created catastrophe in Yugoslavia.

For example, why are UN relief workers assisting the NATO strategy of moving refugees, ethnic Albanians and others, away from the regions bordering Kosovo against their will. The UN's claim that there are "more resources" for them in the areas south of NATO's invasion-staging area is clearly a lie as the organization's own statements on the size of available relief funds demonstrate. (See "Compassion for the refugees" - May 11, 1999)

A possible answer dropped into my mailbox this afternoon from this week's edition of "Focus on the Corporation."

THE UN GOES TO MARKET

It used to be that the United Nations was a thorn in the side of multinational corporations. No more.

Earlier this year, UN Secretary General Kofi Annan called for a partnership to be forged between the UN and global business. To defeat an emerging backlash against economic globalization, big corporations should work with the UN to devise ways to operate responsibly in the Third World, he said.

"Unless [human rights, labor rights and environmental] values are really seen to be taking hold, I fear we may find it increasingly difficult to make a persuasive case for the open global market," he told business leaders at the Davos forum in Switzerland in January.

In February, Annan and the International Chamber of Commerce issued a joint statement in which they declared, "The United Nations and the business community should work jointly to expand economic opportunities, especially in countries which may face marginalization." The joint statement called on the UN and corporations to develop "partnerships" to advance this agenda.

In March, the San Francisco-based Transnational Resource and Action Center (TRAC) revealed what those partnerships may look like in practice, as it released documents describing the UN Development Program's proposed Global Sustainable Development Facility (GSDF).

The GSDF is a fuzzily defined program that seeks to promote corporate investment in sustainable projects in the world's poorest countries. The goal, according to UN officials, is to capture the "positives" of multinational corporations (technology, resources, expertise) and to help promote experimental, innovative, replicable projects that integrate marginalized populations into the global economy. Above all, UN officials hope these projects will create jobs, directly and by employing local parts and service suppliers.

The plan has not taken final shape. Since TRAC released details of the plan, UN officials have said corporations will exert significantly less control over the GSDF than earlier documents indicated. UN officials say they hope to see the GSDF function as a kind of consulting firm to multinationals.

What is clear is that the GSDF has picked shockingly poor corporate candidates for its partnership efforts. Most notable is Rio Tinto, a UK-based mining giant which has compiled a stunning record of violating the very human rights, labor and environmental principles the GSDF is designed to promote. In South Africa-occupied Namibia in the 1980s, for example, the company mined in contravention of numerous UN resolutions and amidst charges that it subjected black miners to horrible workplace and housing conditions. The company has been rocked by protests in Papua New Guinea, Indonesia, Australia, the United States and elsewhere.

Other dubious corporate partners in the GSDF program include Dow Chemical, Citibank and Asea, Brown Boveri, a Swiss-Swedish company which is helping to build some of the most controversial large dams in the world.

UN "partnership" with such corporate rogues is a stark reversal from a decade ago.

In the 1970s and into the 1980s, Third World countries used the UN as a forum in which to call for a New International Economic Order, with economic power and technology transferred from multinationals to developing countries. The UN Center on Transnational Corporations (CTC) did important investigative work on the multinational corporate control over different industries, and advised Third World governments on how to negotiate with multinationals. And for more than 15 years, the CTC oversaw negotiations of a Code of Conduct for Transnational Corporations -- an effort sabotaged and ultimately stifled by the United States on behalf of multinationals. Now, in another sign of the UN's transformation, the CTC has been merged into another UN agency, which tries to promote corporate investment in developing countries.

UN officials are embracing partnerships with multinationals in part out of frustration with the considerable failure of development efforts over the past several decades and in part because they think they have no choice.

But development failures can, to a considerable extent, be traced to too much corporate influence, not too little. Coke is available in poor rural areas in the Third World, but not clean water. Mines, such as those operated by Rio Tinto, despoil the land and water which is central to the livelihood of poor communities. Corporate-driven globalization (assisted by agents like the International Monetary Fund) has pushed countries to grow luxury crops for consumption abroad, not staples to feed the hungry at home.

The Third World does not need UN agencies to facilitate further multinational corporate intrusions into developing countries. Business is quite able to identify investment opportunities without any assistance from the UN, which is much more likely through its GSDF to provide image-enhancement services to big corporations than it is to spark meaningful new job-creating investments.

For the UN, the goal should not be partnership, but independence. Its crucial role should be to help counteract the immense power of multinationals in an increasingly globalized and corporatized economy -- one that is creating unparalleled material wealth but is systematically pushing billions of people into economic despair.

***

Russell Mokhiber is editor of the Washington, D.C.-based Corporate Crime Reporter. Robert Weissman is editor of the Washington, D.C.-based Multinational Monitor. They are co-authors of Corporate Predators (Monroe, Maine: Common Courage Press)

Chinese Embassy Attack No Accident

May 11, 1999

Jared Israel of Counterpunch is the first journalist I am aware of to: 1) study the internal inconsistencies of NATO's explanation of how they "accidentally" attacked the embassy of Yugoslavia's most powerful political ally killing three journalists in three different apartments and 2) present the public with a detailed history of the building and the site where it is located.

Some things to consider:

1. The embassy was not hit by a "dumb" bomb which just happened to drift off target. It was hit by not one, but three different "smart" weapons (the Pentagon won't identify the type) - and each one hit the apartment of a different Chinese journalist.

2. Prior to the building of the embassy, the lot was occupied by a park so it is impossible that there was ever a map - old, new or otherwise - that showed *any* building at this site.

3. A description of the site: "The embassy stands alone in its own grounds surrounded by grassy open space on three sides. Rows of high-rise apartment blocks are located

200 (600 feet) metres away and a line of shops, offices and apartments sits about 150 meters (450 feet) away on the other side of a wide tree-lined avenue, [called]... Cherry Tree Street." (Reuters, 5/8)

Very unlikely to be mistaken for an ammunition warehouse.

4. The Pentagon's own descriptions of how they select and prepare for targets:

"'Target identification and pilot preparation would have been extensive in this case, because of the military importance of the intended target and because Belgrade is heavily defended by Serb forces,' [Air Force Maj. Gen. Charles Wald, a strategic planner for the Joint Chiefs of Staff] said at a briefing for reporters.

"'The way targeting works... the higher the threat, the more valued the target, the more time you would study it. The more time you have to study it, the better,' Wald said."

The use of three, very expensive "smart" weapons would tend to indicate that the target was highly "valued" and there would have been ample time to study it. Remember too, this mistake was not made in the heat of battle. It was, by the Pentagon's own description, a carefully calculated attack that hit its intended targets - three suites in the "wrong" office building.

Israel asks: "What is the likelihood of NATO picking target coordinates that just happen to coincide with three apartments occupied by journalists? I mean, one computer-guided bomb destroying a journalist's home would not be unlikely. But three hitting three journalists' homes?"

If Israel's analysis is correct, and I can't find a flaw in it, then the US is playing a game so reckless as to defy comparison with just about anything that has happened this century. And why? For what?

A long time in the making

May 12, 1999

The current demonstration of merciless terror and violence directed against Yugoslavia makes sense as part of a larger US plan I only just heard about for the first time in this important article, written well before the NATO assault began: "NATO and Beyond" By Ellan Ray and Bill Schaap, Covert Action Quarterly

"Washington is forging ahead with complex, ambitious, and risky plans, if not to supplant, at least to rival NATO, whenever it balks at American cowboy operations. The program is already well entrenched in Eastern Europe, where the Pentagon has bilateral military programs in 13 countries. Plans to expand into the Caucasus and former Soviet Asia are in the works."

An obvious first "exercise" for this group would be the military occupation of one of the few political entities in the region not willing to play ball with NATO. It looks like the nearly century old obsession to contain Russia by any means necessary is still alive and well, making the destruction of one of its staunchest allies in the region a high priority item.

From another article:

"As the war in Bosnia-Herzegovina got underway in mid-1992, American journalists who repeated unconfirmed stories of Serbian atrocities could count on getting published, with a chance of a Pulitzer prize. Indeed, the 1993 Pulitzer Prize for international reporting was shared between the two authors of the most sensational "Serb atrocity stories" of the year: Roy Gutman of Newsday and John Burns of the New York Times. In both cases, the prize-winning articles were based on hearsay evidence of dubious credibility."

Source: Seeing Yugoslavia Through a Dark Glass: Politics, Media, and the Ideology of Globalization - Diana Johnstone Covert Action Quarterly

***

More on the Chinese Embassy mystery:

Another timely analysis of the cover story:

www.wsws.org/articles/1999/may1999/bomb-m10.shtml

The changing tune

May 12, 1999

Yesterday, Agence France Presse, the French news agency, reported on the UN's heavy handed and unpopular attempt to move Kosovo refugees away from the Kosovo-Albanian border deeper into Albania. Unpersuaded by the scare tactics employed (the refugees were told they were in danger of Serb artillery), the overwhelming majority rejected the idea of moving further away from their homes.

The following day, NATO Secretary General Javier Solana, "paid a lightning visit to a Kosovar refugee camp" - one in the *central* part of Albania - and took part in an event reminiscent of an American football rally.

"Dressed in shirtsleeves and looking relaxed and smiling, Solana was met by a loud burst of applause from the refugees, who chanted 'NATO, NATO!' 'KLA, KLA!' and 'USA, USA!'"

Source: Yahoo! News

***

ROBERT NAIMAN

Naiman, who is research associate with the Preamble Center, has organized a petition of American Jews urging the Green Party of Germany (which is part of the coalition government and is meeting tomorrow) to oppose the war and reject analogies to the Nazi Holocaust. The petition, signed by over 200 prominent American Jews, states: "The Holocaust is being invoked in order to justify an unjust bombing campaign against the civilian population of Yugoslavia. Many of us have friends who lost family members in the Holocaust, or have lost relatives ourselves. We are deeply aware of our own history and the need for the world community to intervene in situations where there is a threat of genocide, in order to prevent it. However, this is clearly not what is happening in Yugoslavia today. We do not believe that our government's war against Yugoslavia is motivated by humanitarian concerns. This is evidenced by their refusal to airlift food and water to desperate refugees within Kosovo, as well as the paltry sums allocated for refugee relief as compared to the billions of dollars spent on the bombing. The Clinton Administration's great reluctance to pursue a negotiated solution to the conflict also indicates that this intervention is mainly about power: showing the world that the United States (and NATO, which it largely controls) is the self-appointed international policeman, and stands above international law..."

More on this:

If NATO had been serious about helping ethnic Albanians in Yugoslavia, it would have taken the billions of dollars it has used to rain destruction on the civilian population of Yugoslavia and used it to fund adequate housing and interim supplies for the refugees to sustain themselves in northern Albanian.

Then all that would have been necessary would have been to advise those who were fearful of where to go, a communications project that could have been accomplished for a few million dollars total. Notice that even in its most outlandish propaganda, NATO has never claimed that ethnic Albanians have been prevented from leaving the country.

Instead, as the UN reported yesterday, less than $100 million TOTAL has been put up by member nations to help the refugees.

Whose tail is wagging the dog?

May 13, 1999

RE: CHINESE EMBASSY BOMBING

"We find it unnerving that... offensive capabilities are under the control of an agency... which operates unchecked by our elected representatives and beyond all traditional restraints."

- Edward Eskelson and Tom Bernard,former military Communications Technicians quoted by the Denver Post regarding the still not entirely explained circumstances surrounding how a Korean airliner came to be shot down in Northeast Asia in 1983.

***

There's only one organization on earth that has the ability to:

1. Identify the apartments of specific individuals within a foreign embassy.

2. Insert the coordinates of those locations into a Pentagon pilot's "hit list" without being questioned.

3. Remain completely and irrevocably anonymous while the President, the Pentagon, NATO, and the CIA take the heat for the "mistake" and possibly remain genuinely bewildered and/or misled as to how it happened.

US military people have long complained (privately) of being used by the NSA as "taxi drivers" i.e. being directed to carry out NSA business that is disguised as a Pentagon-managed operation. For example, when an NSA operative is aboard a Navy ship, it is the operative - regardless of his visible rank - not the captain, who calls the shots. He does so by controlling the flow of encrypted communications to and from the ship.

Some public facts about the NSA:

* Signed into being by presidential order by Harry Truman in November 1952, his last major act as president.

* The text of the order remains classified over 40 years later

* Employs more people than "the rest of the intelligence community put together" source: James Bamford ("The Puzzle Palace")

* In 1959, the organization received an additional layer of security through Section 6 of Public Law 86- 36: "Nothing in this Act or any other law... shall be construed to require the disclosure of the organization of any function of the National Security Agency, or any information with respect to the activities thereof, or the names, title, salaries of number of persons employed by the Agency"

In other words, we don't know what they do, how they do it, who they do it to, why they do it and how many people and resources they've got to do it with - and we may never know.

Which explains why the process and personnel behind the targeting of the Chinese embassy, like so many other mysteries of post War US history, may never be credibly disclosed (though bright minds are hard at work at a plausible cover story as we speak - no doubt we'll soon be shown a pseudo-technical explanatory diagram in the New York Times that "explains everything").

If this was an NSA orchestrated hit, why? I can think of a dozen or more motives, but they'd just be guesses. But if you find the tracks of an elephant in your backyard...

In any event, the peace process, such as it was, has been derailed; NATO immediately increased its already obscene level of general bombardment and civilian targeting; and China and Russia have been shown that the US is capable of using reckless violence against them as well as Yugoslavia, like the preferred tactic of the Joe Pesci character in the movie "Goodfellas." Recall that just a few weeks ago, NATO's "supreme commander" was publicly advocating the bombing Russian ships. The actual, "accidental" bombing of the Chinese embassy is the next logical step up from that level of madness.

The official line is the Chinese are *supposed* to believe the bombing was an accident. Anything else is just "whacky" according to one of the US papers best known for being co-opted by US intelligence.

Sayeth the Washington Post:

"Conspiracy theories have always had great currency in Chinese society, in part because of people's restricted access to information. But the conspiracy theories stemming from the embassy attack border on the wacky."

Techniques used so far by the Pentagon news service (CNN, the New York Times, AP etc.) to discredit The Chinese and other skeptics:

#3 characterize the charges as "wild rumors,"

#5 call the skeptics "conspiracy theorists,"

#6 impugn motives,

#7 invoke authority,

#9 come half-clean, and

#13 change the subject. *Anything* but report the facts and address the issues.

For more on this see "13 Techniques of Truth Suppression" by David Martin. (www.brasscheck.com/martin.html)

Further information about the NSA, its strategy, tactics, and operations (such as they can be discerned):

* "The Puzzle Palace" by James Bamford Boston: Houghton Mifflin 1982

* "The Codebreakers" by David Kahn London: Widenfield and Nicolson, 1967

* "The Pueblo Surrender: A Covert Action by the National Security Agency" by Robert A. Liston New York: Bantam Books, 1988 (Most useful for gaining insight into the NSA's ability to manipulate the military and its willingness to engage in dangerous brinkmanship in dealings with China and Russia.)

Battling for the truth

May 13, 1999

"In our time, political speech and writing are largely the defense of the indefensible..."

- George Orwell

***

The daily reports from www.keepfaith.com continue to be exemplary. If nothing else, let as many people as possible know about the daily reports from this courageous 74 year old reporter. It's the best way to keep up with the human reality of what's going on in Yugoslavia.

Today, she's pointed to this site: www.yuheritage.com an ongoing list of the cultural heritage sites that have been damaged or destroyed by bombing so far. I guess what the Nazis didn't accomplish, NATO is going to finish. The extent of damage to churches, monasteries, and other landmarks has not even been hinted at by the US press.

We have archived two of the pages here in case the site goes down:

www.brasscheck.com/yugo/intermap.htm

www.brasscheck.com/yugo/list.htm

***

Secretary of State Albright, whose Jewish family was rescued from the Nazis and supported by a Serbian family during World War II, is actively discouraging members of Congress who are attempting to put forward a reasonable peace plan.

11 members of Congress from various parties and viewpoints have come together to endorse the plan that includes an immediate halt to the bombing.

"The proliferation of congressional diplomatic forays over the past month has surprised many experts -- International Relations Committee Chairman Benjamin A. Gilman (R-N.Y.) said he could not "recall a situation" like this in recent history -- and raised questions about foreign policy leadership on both Capitol Hill and at the White House."

Source: Washington Post

***

The French writer and activist Regis Debray, who was jailed in Bolivia for fighting alongside Che Guevara, has just returned from a week long tour of Yugoslavia:

"On the 'genocide of Kosovars,' Debray notably cited Los Angeles Times correspondent Paul Watson as saying that arson, looting and murder erupted in the first three days of the strikes -- March 24 to 26 -- but that 'he had found no trace since of a crime against humanity.'

Debray said he and others believed Serb forces drove Kosovar Albanians out in the first days when KLA snipers went into action in Pristina and that "uncontrolled" forces staged acts of repression 'probably with the complicity of local police.'"

Source: Yahoo! News

***

Human Rights Watch has expressed its concern about NATO's tactics in a letter to Secretary General Javier Solana.

"Among recent incidents giving rise to these concerns are: the destruction of factories and other property belonging to political supporters of Yugoslav President Slobodan Milosevic; attacks on Yugoslavia's electrical transformers; the destruction of several of Yugoslavia's television and radio stations; several bombings of civilian objects such as the May 7 bombing of the civilian hospital in Nis and the Chinese Embassy in Belgrade, and the bombing of civilian vehicles because they were mistaken for military vehicles or were crossing bridges or near other installations at the time they were attacked."

The UN finally starts to wake up

May 13, 1999

To give you some idea of how thoroughly propagandized top UN officials have been regarding this war, it took a trip to the war zone before UN High Commissioner for Human Rights Mary Robinson *finally* realized today that:

1. "...the range of targets seems very broad and quite clearly civilian residences, hospitals, schools have felt the effects of the bombing."

2. "...there are civilian casualties, there are hospitals where there have been direct hits, I saw the damage to infrastructure, I heard the concerns yesterday evening about ecological damage."

She only just heard concerns about ecological damage *yesterday*?!

Chemical plants and oil refineries have been bombed and radioactive rounds made of "depleted" uranium have been used extensively by NATO. The ecological aspect of this story is, in the scope of events, already very old news. It even made it to mainstream US papers.

3. "Robinson said she had seen children playing among unexploded cluster bombs outside their homes on her visit to the southern Serbian town of Nis, which has suffered civilian casualties in intensive bombing raids by NATO.

'There is no target of any kind in the vicinity and it's happening again and again. It is very worrying. It is not acceptable that civilians are so much in the front line.'"

Better late than never, and this last observation is important, but what in God's name has the UN High Commissioner for Human Rights been occupying herself with for the last 51 days that she is just learning of these things now?

Note: One payload of cluster bombs costs approx. $2.8 million. The TOTAL amount the UN has collected for refugee aid: less than $80 million.

***

The Germans aren't buying it either (maybe)

"The German government of Chancellor Schroder is not satisfied with the explanation given by Washington that bombing of the Chinese embassy was purely a map error and believes that the maps were indeed up-to-date and did show the embassy." (Source: www.inet.co.yu)

I haven't been able to find confirmation of this story, but the above source was among the very first, and among the most thorough, in reporting the details of the bombing of the embassy.

***

Meanwhile US Apache attack helicopters have been moved to the Kosovo border where they engaged in a live fire exercise, but it looks like the latest version of the GE powered, Boeing-manufactured craft doesn't work too well - which is the only explanation for the delay in using them as they were used to fire the *first* shots in the Gulf War.

According to the AFP two have already crashed:

"The failure of a tail rotor is the likely cause of the crash of an AH-64 Apache helicopter in Albania that killed its two crew members, while the loss of a second Apache was the result of pilot error, a Pentagon official said."

This is typical of the Pentagon-establishment and their media friends: they'd sooner admit to the slaughtering of innocents than admit one of their expensive weapon systems doesn't work.

An honest journalist: "We all more or less lied about the war."

May 14, 1999

It's a rare journalist who has the integrity to admit to being duped by propaganda. George Seldes, one of America's most respected journalists and new media critics, talks about his experience covering World War I, the first time the United States became involved in a European war:

"Of the first war years I will say just this: I made a total fool of myself when I accepted as true the news reports from New York and Europe which by their volume and repetition overwhelmed what little objective intelligence I had...

...there was the Lusitania. All the Allied reports told of a "dastardly" and "heinous" crime against civilians, but the German news bureau said the ship carried munitions. Today the sworn statement of the former Collector of the Port of New York, Dudley Field Malone, gives the exact character and tonnage of these munitions, but in 1915 I played the Allied side. I used all the stories of German atrocities including the Baltimore preacher's "unimpeachable" account of the crucifixion of Canadian soldiers by the enemy. In short, in common with about ninety per cent of the American press, I had become a blind but willing agent of the powerful and finally victorious Allied propaganda machine.

...It was not until December, 1918, when I came into Coblenz with the American Army that I realized how fooled I had been by all those years of poisonous propaganda...

...At that time we considered ourselves the most favored and on our return we found ourselves the most envied of mortals, and the journals which printed our stories boasted of the fact their own representatives had been at the fighting front. I now realize that we were told nothing but buncombe, that we were shown nothing of the realities of the war, that we were, in short, merely part of the great Allied propaganda machine whose purpose was to sustain morale at all costs and help drag unwilling America into the slaughter.

...We all more or less lied about the war."

From "One Man's Newspaper Game," Part 1, Chapter 1, in Freedom of the Press, by George Seldes (Garden City, N.Y.: Garden City Publishing Co., Inc., 1937), p. 31-37. Original Copyright 1935, Bobbs Merrill Company.

George later redeemed himself brilliantly:

www.brasscheck.com/seldes

Seldes was haunted his entire life by his failure to report the facts about WWI in a timely way. In his defense, when he and some fellow journalists were finally able to break away from their handlers and actually see some of the reality of the war, General Pershing personally threatened them with a firing squad.

"The propeller fell off"

May 14, 1999

"I interviewed some of these refugees two days ago. When I interviewed the refugees, I found some things to be tremendously interesting. They all said the same thing: In fact, they didn't have any problems until the bombing started."

- Senator James Inhofe (April 29, 1999)

***

For the first time in 41 years of piloting his own plane, a propeller fell off Senator James Inhofe's airplane. It happened last Saturday. I just learned about it today.

Readers who have been following these posts from the beginning know that Senator Inhofe has visited Yugoslavia personally and been an outspoken critic of the bombing. He's also expressed doubt on the veracity of NATO's claim that "the Serbs" are responsible for the mass exodus from Kosovo. He attributes the Albanians' leaving to what he says refugee camps residents told him unanimously: They had no problems until the bombs started dropping.

Inhofe's comments have been all but censored from the US news media, though the transcript of his remarks is available in the Congressional Record and his web site.

Inhofe is Chairman of the Senate Armed Services Readiness Subcommittee.

Details about Inhofe's recent aircraft mishap:

Sen. Jim Inhofe, a pilot for 41 years, made an emergency landing early Saturday after the propeller fell off his airplane.

Inhofe (R-Okla.), was not injured, but his single-engine airplane was slightly damaged, said press secretary Danny Finnerty. Inhofe was alone in the aircraft.

Inhofe said he glided for about eight miles before landing the plane at Claremore Airport. He said he took off from Ketchum, where he keeps his 1979 Grumman Tiger, and had been in the air about 10 minutes when trouble began.

"I noticed a vibration," he said, then heard a pop as the propeller dropped off.

The plane became tail heavy and he knew it would be a difficult landing. "I wasn't sure I could make it," he said.

Inhofe, an experienced, commercially rated pilot, was en route from northeastern Oklahoma to Oklahoma City, where he was to meet the President, who was touring tornado-ravaged parts of central Oklahoma.

Finnerty said the FBI has been asked to investigate because "propellers don't just fly off airplanes every day."

***

Michael Parenti and Peggy Norton treated the death-by-airplane accident of labor leader Walter Reuther at some length in Parenti's book "Dirty Truths." Reuther was an outspoken opponent of the war in Vietnam and Cambodia and despised by Richard Nixon. Parenti's account is well worth reading.

Nearly 30 years later after his death in 1970, the FBI still refuses to turn over nearly 200 pages of documents regarding Reuther's death.

***

"The labor movement is about changing society... What good is a dollar an hour more if your neighborhood is burning down? What good is another $100 pension if the world goes up in atomic smoke?"

- Walter Reuther, founding member of the United Auto Workers

NATO chief: We have no atrocity evidence

May 17, 1999

Three numbers we rarely hear mentioned:

* Number of Serbs killed in concentration camps by Nazi-allied Croatians during WWII: Over 1,000,000

* Total number of people, including KLA and KLA supporters, killed in military actions during the Kosovo civil war in the year preceding the US-lead NATO invasion: 2,000 (US State Department)

* Number of civilians killed by NATO bombing since March 24, 1999: 1,000 (approximate) and growing.

Source: www.counterpunch.org

***

But we'll probably find some *some* day...

The utter lack of hard evidence of Yugoslavian government sponsored atrocities - which is not the same as saying there have been none - was finally acknowledged Sunday by NATO Secretary-General Javier Solana.

(Reuters) "NATO Secretary-General Javier Solana said Sunday he expected to learn 'dramatic facts' surrounding alleged atrocities in Kosovo once international troops had escorted refugees home."

How do you like the spin on that? Didn't we start this noble war to stop known atrocities? Now we have to wait until after the war to find out *if* there were any? This is NATO speaking now, not the German Foreign Affairs Office, or Senator Inhofe, or Regis Debray, or "Serb propaganda."

Currently, there's only one source of atrocity in Yugoslavia that is beyond question:

(AP) "There have been perhaps hundreds of innocent casualties as a result of NATO action," (US) Albright and Cook wrote. "We deeply regret that... But in a conflict as intense as this, it is impossible to eliminate such casualties."

Yugoslavian government spokesmen are claiming, credibly I think, that NATO bombing is making their further withdrawl from Kosovo impossible. And now the *second* convoy of Albanians attempting to return to their homes in Kosovo has been attacked by NATO planes.

In the second, most recent case, Korisa village, in which over 80 refugees were killed, NATO first publicly cast doubt on the story by suggesting the deaths were caused by Serb artillery: "'I would urge all of you to treat with the most high degree of skepticism possible reporting by Serb television in general and with specific reference to this incident,' the State Department's James Rubin told reporters."

When a French journalist found evidence of the remains of NATO weaponry on the scene, NATO then admitted to the bombing, but declared that the 500 refugees and their farm equipment was within a "legitimate target" area.

(Acording to this logic, NATO's strategy now includes bombing areas that they say the Yugoslavs are shelling and the Yugoslavs are shelling their own positions.)

Now, after a day of aggressive spin doctoring, Secretary of State Cohen had this to say about the matter on a General Electric-owned Sunday news program:

"For the Serbs to lament publicly about the deaths of these refugees is almost tantamount to Adolf Eichmann complaining about Allied forces bombing the crematoriums," he said.

However, like Mr. Cohen, NATO Secretary-General Javier Solana, has no evidence of Yugoslavian government atrocities to offer either.

Let's look at this: Lacking *any* evidence, Cohen, a chief spokesman for the US, is perfectly comfortable - in order to justify killing civilians - to equate the children and grandchildren of Nazi-Croat death camp victims with the very same people who arranged for their murder.

How much lower can the individuals responsible for this war sink?

***

On the still-grounded Apache attack helicopters: 24 were sent over. Two have already crashed in training.

The mountains of Yugoslavia are not the easy sand flats of Iraq. And the Yugoslavian army - the grandsons of the farmers who bloodied Hitler's armies - will probably make short work of any that don't crash of their own accord. It's too embarrassing for the Pentagon and their vendors (GE makes the Apache's engine) to admit that the billions of dollars spent building these things produced a weapon that can only shoot at undefended Iraqi positions and conduct urban warfare exercises in US cities. So they sit in Albania until "the time is right."

May that time never come.

***

INSTANT REPLAY

March 13, 1999: "No doubt we'll soon be shown a pseudo-technical explanatory diagram in the New York Times that 'explains everything.'" (About the Chinese Embassy bombing.)

- Brasscheck

You can see it on page 6 of the "Week in Review" section of the Sunday New York Times, March 16, 1999. It explained nothing.

Is it news or propaganda?

May 17, 1999

"Examining the transcripts of two influential (US) TV programs, ABC's "Nightline" and the PBS "NewsHour With Jim Lehrer," FAIR found that only 8 percent of the 291 sources were critics of NATO's bombing. Forty-five percent of sources were current or former U.S. government and military officials, NATO representatives or NATO troops. On "Nightline," the study found, no U.S. sources other than Serbian-Americans were given air time to voice opposition."

Is it news or propaganda?

Cited by Norman Solomon.

Source: www.fair.org

Every ground war needs an "incident"

May 19, 1999

Is there a ground war in the works? Some ominous signs on the propaganda front:

* The AP, which has functioned like a NATO public relations firm throughout the war, has virtually stopped all stories of civilian casualties and replaced them with ones claiming the "effectiveness" of the bombing.

* For the last few days, multivarious "ground war" stories have taken over the headlines: "Blair says now" "Clinton says no" "Clinton says maybe" "What about the Apache helicopters?" and on and on.

* The details of the suffering of refugees in woefully underfunded NATO refugee camps - which have been previously ignored - are now being highlighted, particularly by the AP, as a motivation for "doing something" to repatriate them. (The absurdity of using additional aggression to repatriate people who left their homes as a result of NATO bombing has not been raised.)

* The small stream of pseudo-atrocity stories is accelerating. Most recently a group of male Albanian refugees said they were "roughed up" by Yugoslavian police.

If true, it's contemptible behavior to be sure, but recall that in New York City incidents like this are a *daily* occurrence for minorities and make headlines only in the most extreme cases, such as when an unarmed man with no criminal record or behavior was shot down with an excess of 30 bullets. Or when police were caught red handed torturing a man by sodomizing him with a mop handle. (Both cases are currently in the court system.)

In summary, reports that would implicate NATO in atrocities are being eased out of the US public's consciousness while motivations for and the idea of the "normality" of a ground invasion is being methodically introduced.

All that's needed now is an "incident" to galvanize US public opinion.

Contrary to fraudulent US news polls, most US citizens, far from being in favor of the assault on Yugoslavia, either admit they don't understand what's going on, or are opposed to it.

History has shown it takes the illusion of a terrible atrocity or an imminent threat to American safety to persuade US citizens to support a war.

In previous military assaults, the necessary "incidents" have been simply made up. Some recent examples:

In Sudan, a $100,000,000 pharmaceutical plant was destroyed because it was said to be manufacturing "nerve gas." The charge has since been dropped and $25 million of the owner's money seized by the US has been returned - 18 months later.

In Panama, long-time CIA asset and George Bush colleague Manuel Noriega was declared an international drug dealer and US special operations units fanned out through Panama creating "incidents." (ex. taking shots at US military installations and, dressed in civilian clothes, provoking the Panamanian military into aggressive acts "against American citizens.")

In Grenada, the US claimed the island had been turned into a storehouse for Communist weaponry and that an airfield under construction there was being built to stage attacks on the US. No weapons were found. The airport was in fact being built by European investors to stimulate the tourist trade.

In Vietnam, there was the Tonkin Gulf incident in which Lyndon Johnson falsely claimed that the North Vietnamese attacked US Navy warships thus starting the official US military assault against Vietnam.

If the US decides on a ground war, there *must* be an incident to trigger it. What form will the triggering incident for the next escalation of the war take?

Here's a report on a technique that has already been used successfully against Yugoslavia:

April 28, 1999 (Brasscheck)

CNN: The New Hearst

(Note: William Randolph Hearst openly bragged about using false reports in his newspapers to help start the Spanish-American War.)

The "rationale" for the all-out assault on Yugoslavia, including numerous civilian targets, is that it's needed to stop the atrocities being committed by the Serbs. This one-sided version of events has been promoted non-stop by CNN since the civil war in Bosnia. Here's just one example of the blatant misrepresentation that CNN has engaged in while reporting on the tragic situation in the Balkans.

"... Another big CNN story early in the Bosnian conflict was the killing, allegedly by Serb snipers, of two "Muslim babies" on a bus. Who could not have been horrified by the tragic sight of the funeral service for those innocent Muslim babies?

Where were Ms. Amanpour and CNN to set the record straight? If it had not been for French 2 TV that covered the funeral, this writer would never have known that the babies were Serbian (not Muslim), killed by a Muslim sniper, as was made painfully clear by the presence of a Serbian Orthodox priest conducting the funeral service... before it was interrupted by a grenade attack.

However, in the CNN coverage *the priest had been cropped out*, leaving the American audience to believe that Serbs were not only the assassins, but were also responsible for the grenade attack."

Source: "Odd alliance at State, CNN?" Stella Jatras, The Washington Times. March 14, 1999

***

Note: Ms. Amanpour has recently arrived in Albania.

Another explosive report blacked out by the US news media

May 19, 1999

"...on Wednesday, public relations specialist Leslie Dach was recruited by the White House to help the National Security Council shape its communication strategy about Kosovo. Dach, active in Democratic causes and head of the Washington office of Edelman Public Relations Worldwide, was an outside adviser to Clinton during the impeachment battle. Dach planned to lend his services for 30 days."

- Source: New York Times, May 13, 1999

***

US news consumers may be getting the best (the worst?) that the public relations world has to offer, but they're sure not getting even the most basic facts about the reports on Yugoslavia generated within their own country.

Here's something I only just discovered today - and I had to learn about it from a Yugoslavian news source. If anybody doubts that US news and US propaganda have become one on the subject of this war, look at some of the explosive facts the US news media has not bothered to report.

This information comes from The International Strategic Studies Association (ISSA) which organized a fact-finding mission from Washington DC to Yugoslavia on April 18-21, 1999.

US Congressman Jim Saxton (Republican, New Jersey), an ISSA Life Member and Chairman of the US House of Representatives Task Force on Terrorism & Unconventional Warfare (and member of the House Armed Services Committee; and Vice-Chairman of the Joint [House-Senate] Economic Committee), participated in the mission.

Here's a summary of their report:

* At least 1/3 of all Albanian refugees are fleeing deeper *into* Yugoslavia to avoid the KLA. (Brasscheck note: NATO uses KLA intelligence for planning air strikes which may explain the two "accidental" bombings of Albanian civilians.)

* NATO bombing is a major contributive cause of the suffering of Kosovar Albanians and many other ethnic groups within Yugoslavia as well.

* Yugoslavia is the most multicultural, multi-religious state in the Balkan region and home to 26 different ethnic groups. Only 2/3 of Yugoslavia is Serbian.

* Over 2 million Yugoslavians of all origins have been rendered homeless or income-less as the result of NATO. The country's total population is less than 11+ million.

* NATO bombing has seriously weakened democratic dissent with the Yugolavian Republic and has struck numerous non-military targets (hospitals, churches, schools, food processing plants etc.).

* Many of the economic targets are worker-owned enterprises.

* The extent of NATO equipment and personnel losses to date has been withheld from the public.

Letter from a former Nuremberg prosecutor

May 21, 1999

U.S. AGGRESSION

Letter by Walter J. Rockler, Former prosecutor, Nuremberg war crimes trials:

As the bombs, smart and dumb, fall ceaselessly on Serbs, Montenegrins and sometimes Albanians, on bridges, waterworks, electric generation plants and factories, and on trains, trucks and homes, the remorseless crusade for "humanitarianism" presses forward to the applause of journalistic and academic shills. To paraphrase the Roman historian Tacitus, we are busy creating a desert, which we can then call peace.*

For the United States, alias "NATO," the planning and launching of this war by the president heightens the abuse and undermining of war-making authority under the Constitution. (It seems to be accepted that the president can order his personal army to attack any country he pleases.) The bombing war also violates and shreds the basic provisions of the United Nations Charter and other conventions and treaties; the attack on Yugoslavia constitutes the most brazen international aggression since the Nazis attacked Poland to prevent "Polish atrocities" against Germans. The United States has discarded pretensions to international legality and decency, and embarked on a course of raw imperialism run amok.

Our alleged concern with human rights borders on the ludicrous. We dropped twice as many bombs on Vietnam as all the countries involved in World War II dropped on each other. We killed hundreds of thousands of civilians in the course of that war. Very recently, in Central America, we sponsored, trained and endorsed the local armies--Guatemalan, Salvadoran, and Nicaraguan Contras--in the killing of at least 200,000 people. We encouraged the Pinochet coup in Chile with the resulting killing of another few thousand or so people, including the democratically elected president. We saw nothing wrong with the Croat slaughter and expulsion of 200,000 Serbs from the Krajina area. We have taken very little stand on the monumental slaughters of hundreds of thousands, if not millions, of people in Africa. We have restrained the Iraqis from attacking Kurds but see nothing amiss in Turks attacking Kurds. We cannot even agree to abandon the use of landmines.

In reality when we, the self-anointed rulers of this planet, issue an ultimatum to another country, it is "surrender or die." To maintain our "credibility," we must crush any semblance of resistance to our dictates to that country.

* Brasscheck note:

The quote: "The Romans make a desert and call it peace," is from Galgacus, a Caledonian chieftain, in a speech to his army before meeting the Romans in battle in 86 AD. It's cited in Tacitus' "Life of Agricola."

***

A paper that's changed its tune

A month ago, the New York Observer was describing the bombing of Yugoslav civilians with casual detachment and calling Milosevic one of the greatest mass murderers of the 20th century who must be stopped at any cost.

That rhetoric has disappeared and been replaced by this, from columnist Nicholas von Hoffman. It's an excellent summary of the true moral position of the US in this war:

"In what may come to be called the Coward's War, civilian casualties mount as diplomacy languishes... To these almost daily horrors, the White House-Pentagon-State Department line is to first deny responsibility and then categorize the fussing about them as a Yugoslavian 'public relations offensive.' Similarly, the Serbian refusal to call dead people 'collateral damage' and their persistence in publicizing the gory effects** of our precision bombing is deemed a fraudulently transparent attempt to gain sympathy.

Washington's talk about making war for humanitarian goals has markedly lessened of late. When the slaughter began, Heartfelt Willie's speech was perfumed with the humanitarian sentiments he speaks with such facility. The word, humanitarian, was seldom off the lips of American officialdom, but the emphasis has switched over from aid, comfort, and help to winning. No more sweet talk, now it's crush the enemy, conquer them, and on to victory."

** Brasscheck note: In the process of the war, NATO has destroyed several Yugoslavian television stations and killed and injured numerous journalists both Yugoslav and Chinese. Recently, the US, until caught and stopped, was in the process of forcing Yugoslavia's US-owned commercial Internet access provider to take the nation off the network. Stated goal: to stop "Serbian propaganda."

***

In a visit to Washington yesterday, British Foreign Minister Cook had this to say:

"The U.S.A. should be proud of what it has accomplished in the Kosovo campaign... This is not the time to lose our nerve. The air campaign is working and NATO should be ready to take advantage of its success.

Cook's bottom line: "We can't buckle first" because that would greatly weaken NATO.

So now, we are bombing Yugoslavian civilians to insure the health and longevity of NATO!? By whose authority is this bombing taking place anyway?

NATO press release

22 March 1999

STATEMENT BY THE NORTH ATLANTIC ALLIANCE ON THE SITUATION IN KOSOVO

In response to Belgrade's continued intransigence and repression, the Secretary General of NATO, to whom the North Atlantic Council had delegated on 30 January the authority to decide on air operations, is completing his consultations with the Allies to this end.

In view of the evolution on the ground of the situation in Kosovo, the North Atlantic Council has also authorized today the Secretary General, to decide, subject to further consultations, on a broader range of air options if necessary."

And what were the demands refused by Yugoslavia which the country still deems unacceptable:

"7. NATO personnel shall be immune from any form of arrest, investigation, or detention by the authorities in the FRY (Federal Republic of Yugoslavia.)

8. NATO personnel shall enjoy... free and unrestricted passage and unimpeded access throughout the FRY including associated airspace and territorial waters.

11. NATO is granted the use of airports, roads, rails and ports without payment...

15. [NATO shall have] the right to use all of the electromagnetic spectrum..."

Source: The Rambouillet Text of Feb. 23. Excerpts from Appendix (B)

In other words, an unelected body designated an individual, who is answerable to no electorate, to make the decision on undertaking a massive, violent assault against a sovereign country that has not invaded or threatened to invade any member of NATO. And why? Because NATO wants said country to give its consent to an unlimited military occupation.

The last time such a twisted justification for attacking a European country was invoked, the words came out of the mouth of Adolph Hitler.

That's history folks, like it or not.

NATO's obscured motivation

May 24, 1999

"...the pilots I've talked to are frustrated that people don't understand how well it's going."

- Air Force General Charles Wald as quoted by the Washington Post, May 24th

"..through the ignorant arrogance of the most small-minded, narcissistic, and incompetent western leaders of our lifetime, we find ourselves once again in grave danger of global catastrophe."

- Sam Smith, Progressive Review

***

Apache Brief: Tim Butcher of the London Telegraph has finally reported what I advised readers of these dispatches on May 13. The Apache helicopters sent to Albania - along with 5,000 US troops "to guard them" - will never fly into Kosovo from Albania because they are militarily useless in the face of the region's high mountain terrain.

Yet to reach the public eye: the vulnerability of the "invulnerable" stealth bomber.

***

Is it propaganda or is it news?

A few weeks ago, the Clinton Administration was caught trying to force a US-owned Internet service provider to cut Yugoslavia off the Internet in part to stop you and others from seeing "Serb propaganda" like this, from www.keepfaith.com:

"Please, please do something. You are killing us.

They were hitting power plants, water lines and distribution plants all over Yugoslavia - they still maintain that they don't target civilians. NATO briefings are becoming a joke throughout Europe. The war criminals.

How are we going to live without water?"

- Madame Ivanka Besevi, Age 74

And this one:

"I am back again. We are being rationed, 4 hours on, 4 hours off. This is a catastrophe. I am speechless, people are on the brink of madness, myself included. My elderly mother cannot stop crying. My aunt, who is 80, is in the same condition, being very sound of mind both of them have understood what the USA is trying to do. Kill us all. Little by little, they have been taking away everything we have... My heart is about to explode with worry, despair, incredulity."

- Djordje

As I scan the newspapers and press services, I see no shortage of stories about Albanian refugees (refugees of all other backgrounds are ignored), but virtually nothing about the war's other victims: millions of civilians of Yugoslavia's 26 different ethnic backgrounds who are enduring the most vicious bombing campaign in Europe since World War II.

Cities are losing their water systems, electric service is failing, serious food shortages are developing, and, with the destruction of Yugoslavia's largest pharmaceutical plant, a shortage of medicine is looming.

The goal seems to be to turn Yugoslavia into the next Iraq.

The manic air assault, which has killed well over 1,000 non-combatants and injured thousands of others, will soon eclipse the total death count in the Kosovo civil war between February 1998 and March 1999 which the State Department set at 2,000. And keep in mind, that 2,000 figure includes KLA combatants and their supporters in the midst of an armed insurrection.

Western news services are capable of getting reports from Belgrade and other parts of Yugoslavia. Just days ago much was made of a protest against the government held there. But other than the occasional picture of a deliberately destroyed power plant or an accidentally damaged embassy, the US press treats Yugoslavia as if it were empty, populated only by "targets" and the unfortunate people who find themselves in them - factory workers, journalists, engineers, nurses, patients, children - when they are blown up.

The "success" of NATO? It has finally revealed some figures.

Destroyed or significantly damaged:

70 tanks

130 APCs (armored personnel carriers)

130 artillery

250 trucks

80 planes

31 bridges

2 major roads into Kosovo

That's 660 piece of military equipment (a nice round number by the way). Does that seem like a spectacular military success given that NATO has bombed the country every day in excess of 60 days, many times flying in excess of 500 missions per day?

What NATO *has* been successful in, is destroying the Yugoslavian civilian economy. Several *thousand* dwellings, factories, and industrial facilities have been seriously damaged or destroyed including: oil and chemical refineries and storage fields, fertilizer plants, pharmaceutical plants, food processing plants, a milk cow breeding farm, over one dozen hospitals including a Gerontological Center in Leskovac, hundreds of school buildings, tens of thousands of housing units, and TV and radio broadcast and transmission facilities. Counter Punch has a list of the first month's sickening toll here: www.counterpunch.org/bodycount.html [Original source no longer available.]

Finding hard information on this devastation in the US press is for all practical purposes impossible. Only the most extraordinary events - the two-time air assault on a packed passenger train, the destruction of a hospital, the bombing of the Chinese embassy, the slaughter of Albanian refugees - can grab the US news media's attention and inspire them to go beyond their normal roll of "rip and read" and ask a few pointed questions.

Meanwhile, every injury to an Albanian refugee - "some of the men were roughed up" "we were given only bread and water and an occasional egg" "we were robbed by masked men" "we were told to leave our homes" - deplorable events all - are transformed into detailed, feature news stories in papers like the New York Times on a daily and, in the case of the AP, hourly basis.

This is not journalism. It's propaganda. By shielding US news consumers from the reality of the violence inflicted by NATO, CNN, the AP, the New York Times and all the other news outlets that are treating the war as a spectator event - a kind of serial video war game - and are helping perpetuate the agony.

Instead of the very real topic of the human suffering the bombing is causing, the news media busies itself with speculation about the coming ground war.

And what can stop this madness?

The AP, in a report relayed by the Washington Post, claims that the diplomatic sticking points are as follows:

"Besides demanding that Milosevic withdraw his security forces from Kosovo, NATO is insisting he permit the return of more than 800,000 ethnic Albanian refugees, of the 2.1 million Kosovo pre-war populace, who have fled or been deported."

Given that the vast majority of Albanians - over 90% - who left Kosovo left *after* the NATO bombing began, this is an odd point for the AP to highlight as the reason for the continuation of the bombing.

Odder still is the absolute US news media blackout of the *real* sticking point, the one that triggered the bombing in the first place: NATO's insistence that Yugoslavia submit to a nationwide military occupation and that government's refusal to consent.

The following clauses in the Rambouillet Text bear repeating:

7. NATO personnel shall be immune from any form of arrest, investigation, or detention by the authorities in the FRY (Federal Republic of Yugoslavia).

8. NATO personnel shall enjoy... free and unrestricted passage and unimpeded access throughout the FRY including associated airspace and territorial waters.

11. NATO is granted the use of airports, roads, rails and ports without payment...

15. [NATO shall have] the right to use all of the electromagnetic spectrum...

These extraordinary demands - which any sovereign nation would be obligated to refuse - *not* Yugoslavia's unwillingness to submit to mediation or a legitimate UN peacekeeping force, are the root cause of the dispute which NATO is now attempting to "resolve" through violence, terror, and, at the root of it all, US news media-enabled lying.

What has prevented the US news media from conveying this simple fact?

***

"I really look with commiseration over that great body of my fellow citizens, who, reading newspapers, live and die in the belief that they have known something of what has been passing in the world in their time."

- Thomas Jefferson, letter to John Norvell, June 14, 1807

Back in the saddle

May 25, 1999

"Jane's Defense Weekly, in a very significant story in the May 10 issue, reports that the current leader of the Kosovo Liberation Army is a Croatian general, Agim Ceku. He was in charge of Operation 'Storm,' the bloodiest and most brutal military campaign - until the current NATO bombing - carried out in the Balkans since the invasion of the Nazis during World War II. In August 1995, he began the Operation 'Storm' offensive against the Serbian population in the Krajina region in Croatia, that drove hundreds of thousands of Serbs from the region that they have inhabited for centuries.

Ceku is a U.S.-trained military officer who is closely tied to the Pentagon's Military Professional Resources, Inc. (MPRI). The MPRI is a semi-official Pentagon contractor, headed by retired U.S. military officers. It specializes in sending mercenary armies under Pentagon contract into unofficial wars. The MPRI was contracted by the Pentagon to organize and train the Croatian Army for its Operation Storm against Serbs in Krajina. This massive ground offensive against hundreds of thousands of civilians was seen as the decisive military event that forced the Milosevic government in Yugoslavia to sign the U.S.-brokered Dayton Accord for Bosnia."

Source: Brian Becker, Co-Director, International Action Center "Is the U.S./NATO leadership planning a ground war?"

MPRI's website: www.mpri.com

You can anticipate where America's next major military involvement will be by reading MPRI's "help wanted ads." Hint: Africa.

***

Retired Canadian military officer given platform by the Washington Post to predict a Serb atrocity

"Based on the principle that the best defense is a good offense, it would seem that Milosevic's best option would be an attack, perhaps with artillery and missiles, against the crowded refugee camps on the Kosovo borders."

- Lewis MacKenzie. Commander of U.N. troops during the siege of Sarajevo in the Bosnian war in 1992. Source: The Washington Post, Sunday, May 23, 1999; Page B01

This odd comment comes from a military man who, like Agim Ceku, spent his time in Yugoslavia directing the shelling of areas inhabited by Serb civilians. His suggestion was slipped into a not terribly insightful or enlightening "critique" of NATO. Summary: a) it's not as well organized as the UN was and b) it suffers from too many opinions to be able to carry out a proper war.

But to focus on MacKenzie's statement: If the government of Yugoslavia were of a mind to shell Albanian civilians, why hasn't it done so already? And why, in the middle of a life and death struggle to defend its territory against NATO bombing and KLA terrorism, would it expose itself and commit scarce resources by crossing an international border for the purposes of committing an atrocity in broad daylight.

Clearly, this is the fantasy of a professional Serb hater, and this kind of bizarre projection is more appropriate for the cover of a supermarket tabloid than a newspaper with pretensions of accuracy. Yet there it is, in black and white, an "authority" in a "legitimate" paper stating that the Yugoslavian army's best tactic at this point is to stage an "attack, perhaps with artillery and missiles, against the crowded refugee camps on the Kosovo borders."

Are the professional Serb-haters telegraphing their next move? Is a staged atrocity involving refugees to be blamed on the Yugoslavian government in order to convert popular opinion in favor of a ground invasion?

Interestingly, today NATO announced via an AP report that the policy of using the UN to frighten Albanian refugees into moving away from the border area and deeper into Albania has been dropped. "These people have seen enough violence in Kosovo. They should be treated with respect," NATO spokesman Lt. Col. Helge Eriksen said.

NATO's all heart, isn't it?

If an "atrocity" like the one in McKenzie's fantasies does in fact occur, it will be timed to take place at more or less the same time NATO is prepared to launch its ground invasion. A press pool will just happen to be conveniently nearby and, if the presentation is dramatic enough, it may be used to break into normal TV programming, a la OJ Simpson's non-getaway in the Ford Bronco. Christiane Amanpour is not cooling her jets in Albania for nothing.

Unduly cynical? Only if you don't know how the current air war got started...

***

William Walker and the short memory of the US press

"On January 15, 1999, in the Kosovo village of Racak, Yugoslav and Serbian police forces were accused of carrying out a horrible massacre of civilians. William Walker, a U.S. diplomat in charge of the international monitoring force in Kosovo, went to the site with Western reporters and proclaimed that 45 people had been "killed in the massacre." Pictures of 40 bodies laid out in a village Mosque were put on the front page of all the major Western newspapers. Walker called it a "crime against humanity" by the Yugoslav government led by Slobodon Milosevic...

William Walker was presented as the consummate neutral peace keeper. Why question his word? In fact, no major U.S. media outlet did question his account. William Walker, however, is not a neutral peacekeeper. He is a war criminal and a professional liar. As a special assistant to Lt. Col. Oliver North and Assistant Secretary of State Eliot Abrams, Walker was a key operator in Reagan's White House operation to overthrow the Nicaraguan government in the 1980s.

According to charges filed in U.S. district court by independent counsel Lawrence Walsh, Walker was responsible for setting up a phony humanitarian operation at an airbase in Ilopango, El Salvador. That "humanitarian" air base was used to run guns, munitions, and supplies to the fascist Contra mercenaries attacking the Nicaraguan Revolution. Walker was also the U.S. Ambassador to El Salvador from 1988 to 1992, when military death squads murdered thousands of progressive workers, peasants, and young people...

While the U.S. media accepted Walker's massacre story and used it to create the war hysteria that permitted the current NATO bombing war, many of the European press challenged Walker's and the KLA's account. The French newspapers Le Monde, Le Figario, and Liberation all ran stories pointing out major inconsistencies in the "massacre" report. There was considerable evidence, in fact, that the corpses were not civilians at all, but KLA soldiers who, after having been killed in a battle, had been dressed in civilian garb and placed in the mosque."

Source: "Is the U.S./NATO leadership planning a ground war?" Brian Becker, Co-Director, International Action Center

***

I've seen the pictures from Racak and other sites that used to be trumpeted as "proof" of genocide. All the victims are military-aged men and their bodies have clearly been moved and positioned for the camera. They were definitely not shot where they lay and there is no way, based on the pictures alone, or Mr. Walker's good word, to know who these people were or the circumstances under which they died.

Why haven't American news readers been apprised of these basic realities?

The answer is simple: because rather than inform them, the US news media has chosen - as it has in every other manufactured war - to participate in a choreography of misrepresentation designed to draw Americans, whose families provide the sons and whose taxpayers provide the funds, into throwing their emotional support behind a war they would never approve of if they knew the facts. A war that has the potential to destabilize the world, bankrupt US society, and spill oceans of innocent blood before all its reverberations reach their end...

Agim Ceku, Lewis MacKenzie, William Walker, and others like them can count on press "discretion" when they need it and a platform when they want it.

The results of a study recently conducted by FAIR on press coverage of the NATO bombing bear repeating:

"Examining the transcripts of two influential (US) TV programs, ABC's "Nightline" and the PBS "NewsHour With Jim Lehrer," FAIR found that:

* Only 8 percent of the 291 sources were critics of NATO's bombing.

* Forty-five percent of sources were current or former U.S. government and military officials, NATO representatives or NATO troops.

* On "Nightline," the study found, no U.S. sources other than Serbian-Americans were given air time to voice opposition."

Source: www.fair.org, cited in an article by Norman Solomon.

***

"...if only the press were to do its duty, or but a tenth of its duty, this hellish system could not go on."

- William Cobbett, Rural Rides, 1830

The stats NATO doesn't want you to see

May 26, 1999

"What we are seeing, then, are military actions being launched against often spurious targets for the sake of US domestic political considerations. Once again, this is nothing new and certainly nothing invented by the Clinton Administration. Former US Central Intelligence Agency intelligence professional and writer Miles Copeland many years ago said that US foreign policy is merely domestic policy carried out abroad."

- Gregory Copley ('The Impact of US Domestic Issues on The US and Global Strategic Posture' from "Defense & Foreign Affairs Strategic Policy" 9-10, 1998)

***

Gen. Clark's military "triumphs": the real story

"A Pentagon official said that despite the problems caused to civilians, focusing on the electrical system was a legitimate objective because President Slobadan Milosevic's military operations depend on electricity."

- New York Times May 25, 1999 A-16

By that line of reasoning, the next logical step would be to starve the country and, if possible, remove the oxygen from its air. NATO is working on it.

In an urban environment, taking away electricity takes away safe drinking water; hot water; the ability to prepare and refrigerate food, operate food processing plants like flour mills, light streets, operate traffic signals, use the telephone, run elevators, run air raid signals, etc. The most acute suffering will be seen in hospitals where there will be insufficient water to bathe bed-ridden patients and sterilize instruments.

But, according to NATO, this is not a war against civilians - and the deaths, injuries, and widespread suffering of the 26 ethnic groups that reside in Yugoslavia are unintended.

Accepting this statement at face value, what then exactly has NATO accomplished militarily in its 60+ day bombing campaign? Getting a straight answer to this simple question is difficult if you're watching CNN or reading the Times or the Post, because the answer is embarrassing to the Pentagon and therefore they don't spoon feed it to US reporters.

Here are the numbers:

* Yugoslavia's forces

Source: Jane's 1997 report on Yugoslavian forces:

1,025 MBTs (tanks),

850 ACVs (armored combat vehicles),

3,750 artillery pieces,

155 combat aircraft,

53 attack helicopters

* NATO's claims of military achievement

Source: AP

Destroyed or damaged:

70 tanks (out of 1,025)

130 ACVs (out of 850)

130 artillery (out of 3,750)

80 planes (out of 155)

* About the first month's bombing:

Source: CounterPunch (www.counterpunch.com)

"During the first month of the war on Yugoslavia, the NATO planes and cruise missiles made over 10,000 attacks. More than 2,500 cruise missiles were launched and over 7,000 tons of explosives were dropped."

Note: To calculate NATO's total expenditure in 60 days, double above amounts.

Isn't it odd that such simple, easy to find numbers are never presented in the flood of US war news? Aren't these numbers, in fact, *the* war news?

Why such an abysmal performance by NATO? Because tanks, artillery, and ACVs are the easiest things in the world to hide. They can be put in caves, barns, warehouses, truck trailers, underground parking lots, covered with camouflage and stashed in the woods, or just put under tarps. Hiding equipment is basic military procedure. NATO knew this going into this "war."

What is also basic military procedure is to not return to base with a plane load full of undropped bombs. Why? It's hazardous to land with them onboard.

So what are the intrepid NATO pilots doing when they can't find legitimate targets to hit? Dumping them anywhere they can as they head back to base. Recently, an Italian fisherman was seriously wounded when his net picked up a freshly dumped US-manufactured munition.

Source: SF Bay Guardian

Nicolas von Hoffman of the New York Observer hit the nail on the head when he called this the Coward's War.

However, it may be even worse than that.

Counter Punch reports that General Wesley Clark was commander of the Cavalry Division of the III Corps at Fort Hood. That's the Army base that provided the equipment and personnel for the incineration of the Branch Davidian compound at Waco Texas.

The CounterPunch story is especially chilling when one considers the evidence that's come out since that shows the US military had a strong presence at Waco by day two, and possibly as early as day one, if not sooner:

"Even before the raid, members of the US Armed Forces, many of them in civilian dress, were around the compound."

Clinton now in violation of the War Powers Act

May 26, 1999

As of today, President Clinton is now in violation of the 1973 War Powers Resolution, the one created to prevent another Vietnam War. He is, in essence, now using the US military to pursue a purely personal agenda without the Constitutionally required approval of Congress. He is the first president to overtly violate this law since its passage.

26 members of Congress have filed a lawsuit in federal court today to have the law enforced and the military assault ended. The 60 day period a president has to use the military without Congressional approval ended last night at midnight. (More on this at end of dispatch.)

This should have been front page news in every newspaper in the US and the lead story of every news broadcast. Was it even reported? The AP ignored it. So did Reuters. Instead they reported "record bombing" by NATO.

***

From Keep Faith (www.keepfaith.com)

"Over 10,000 bombs fell on Yugoslavia. NATO admits to only 9 mistakes. Congratulations. I don't know if this is interesting enough for you to publish, but it's our current situation."

"Prianovici, near Pozega in Serbia, is mentioned in almost every bombing report. No one knows why they are getting bombed as much as they do. There's only some 200 families living in this farming village, trying to farm between the bombings - the only thing standing between all of us and starvation come winter.

"We don't really know how many were exterminated, as the smoking ruins of the homes, hospitals and businesses are still being sifted for the victims. We might never know, as the new, exciting weapons NATO experiments with have a tendency to destroy human bodies in such untidy ways (except, God help us, the thermal bombs that are self-contained crematoriums) that it's sometimes impossible to sort the shreds of bone and flesh enough for a countdown."

Madame Ivanka Besevic, 74, retired journalist reporting daily from Belgrade

***

PRESIDENT CLINTON IS NOW USING THE MILITARY IN DIRECT VIOLATION OF ALL US LAW

FOR RELEASE:

May 26, 1999

Clinton in violation of law

Had 60 days to pull-out of Kosovo or get approval -- neither has happened

WASHINGTON, DC -- As of 12:01 am Wednesday, May 26, President Clinton will be in clear violation of the 1973 War Powers Resolution. This is the first time a president has violated the resolution since its enactment.

"President Clinton has nothing left to claim: he is in complete violation of the War Powers Resolution, there is simply no other interpretation," said US Rep. Ron Paul (R, Texas).

Rep. Paul is one of 26 Members of Congress who have filed a lawsuit in federal court against President Clinton in regards to his violation of the War Powers Resolution and the US Constitution.

"No one can argue that a president must, when there is a direct, clear and present danger to American lives, take defensive actions to protect our national interest. However, 60 days ago this president decided to take aggressive action against a sovereign nation; and has since had congressional authorization rejected by a vote of 427 to 2," said Rep. Paul.

"Under the War Powers Resolution, a president may engage in hostilities for 60 days without congressional approval. At the end of the 60-day period, however, the president must have either received a Declaration of War, received authorization to continue the action for another set period of time, or begin withdrawing the troops. Since the bombing of Yugoslavia began, the president has been denied a declaration of war and authorization.

"Once again, though, President Clinton is demonstrating his utter disregard for the Constitution and laws of this nation. He apparently views himself as a king, rather than the president of a constitutional republic; he must believe that his will is the law, rather than the Constitution and acts of Congress," said Rep. Paul. "To say this president is anything but dangerous and reckless would be a gross understatement."

Rep. Paul said that while many presidents have violated, with the unspoken consent of Congress, the constitutional responsibility for the initiation of war, President Clinton has done so more frequently and brazenly than any other this century.

"While I am hopeful this president will change his course, recent history has shown this president holds no more respect for court orders than he does for the Constitution or the War Powers Resolution. If he shows the same contempt as in the past, our nation faces serious trouble."

Day Two of the Unconstitutional War

May 27, 1999

Slobodan Milosevic and four powerful aides were indicted today by the UN court. The charges: causing the deportation of 740,000 Kosovo Albanians and for the murder of 340 Kosovo Albanians.

The first charge is bizarre because anyone following the situation knows that the vast majority, over 90%, of the refugees left the country AFTER NATO started bombing, many claiming they were in fear not of "the Serbs" but of NATO.

Another credible report has at least one third of Albanian refugee fleeing Kosovo deeper *into* Yugoslavia to avoid KLA forces which have been known to terrorize them.

As for the murder of 340 Kosovo Albanians, I don't have enough information to comment, but the AP report on the indictment fails to mention if these particular invididuals were: a) armed members of the KLA terrorist group or b) people providing the KLA with logistical support. It makes a difference and I notice the AP report took pains to *not* label them "civilians."

What will the effect of the indictment be?

“Now Milosevic is put into a corner and there's no incentive for him to make a compromise,” said Vojin Dimitrijevic, director of the Belgrade Center for Human Rights. Source: AP

Surely the court must have known that by issuing this indictment they are ensuring further bloodshed.

This is the court of the same organization that claims not to have known civilian targets were being hit by NATO until 51 days into the war and has issued statements that the war has created no ecological threat, though the leaders of neighboring countries have complained about the effect the war is having on *their* environment, hundreds of miles away. Source: Yahoo! News (Original source no longer available.)

Meanwhile President Clinton is in the second day of a blatant violation of the War Powers Act which makes this war indisputably illegal. The "peacekeeping" force on the south border of Yugoslavia will expand to 50,000 and is now being openly described by policy makers as a potential invasion force. The US Air Force has cancelled all retirements and declared Kosovo "a major theater war" - even though war has not been declared, the 60 days given Clinton by the War Powers Act is up, and an apparent majority of Congress is now opposed to the war (16 pro-bombing Democrats have changed their tune).

In the midst of the ongoing madness, some NATO members are making timid requests for restraint.

WASHINGTON (AP) – “Canada is lodging a plea for NATO to choose its bombing targets in Yugoslavia more carefully as the Clinton administration extends its review of U.S. policy in the Kosovo conflict.”

Germany and the Netherlands have extended similar pleas.

Russia, China, and India have called for an immediate end to the bombing as have numerous other countries. On May 25, Russia's Yeltsin went so far as to threaten "reprisals" and "extreme measures" if the assaults on civilians continue. It is within the country's capability to act on these threats.

Let's see: 1) innocent civilians are being killed daily; 2) the life support systems of a nation are being destroyed piece by piece threatening the lives and health of millions; 3) the majority of the world's population is calling for an immediate halt to the bombing; 4) two major military powers, China and Russia, have expressed extreme objections, the latter going so far as to suggest possible reprisals, and 5) the president is acting in direct violation of the War Powers Act and the Constitution.

Not satisfied with destroying the country's electrical and water systems, NATO "voted" yesterday to destroy its telephone and computer communications systems as well.

Source: Washington Post

The evidence for the charges from the UN's court?

"The tribunal has been forced to rely largely on eyewitness accounts from refugees who have poured into neighboring Macedonia and Albania because Belgrade authorities repeatedly have refused to let Arbour or her deputies enter Kosovo."

"The committee had not personally interviewed a single witness. The report was based on 1,200 depositions mostly from refugees, taken by 22 barristers from Britain. None of the witnesses were placed on oath, their names were omitted (to prevent reprisals against their relatives), and hearsay evidence was accepted at full face value... (later) a commission of inquiry... failed markedly to corroborate a single major allegation on the report."

- Phillip Nightly from "The First Casualty"

Posted by Brasscheck April 16, 1999

The above is the historical account of how the United States was drawn into World War One when British propagandists accused - falsely it was proven later - the "Huns" of bayoneting Belgian babies and crucifying Canadian POWs. There is an obvious problem with being drawn into World War Three. At least two of our potential adversaries possess sufficient nuclear weaponry to destroy large sections of our major population centers.

The recklessness of what Clinton, Blair and their controllers are engaged in is unprecedented. And the US news media, with very few exceptions, carries on as if all is well.

Interview with the "bad guy"

May 28, 1999

Some people have asked about the likelihood of NATO being indicted for war crimes for the bombing of civilian targets in Yugoslavia. The UN's chief war-crimes prosecutor answered that question a few days ago:

"(Arbour) said it would be 'wildly premature' for her to speculate on whether accusations that NATO has violated the Geneva Conventions will ever be substantiated."

Source: National Post (Canada) - May 21, 1999

Let's see if I understand this. We can witness with our own eyes the destruction of civilian targets and the slaughter of non-combatants, but these acts, according to the UN's chief prosecutor, are unlikely to ever be "substantiated."

On the other hand, second and third hand refugee stories (some of which may very well be true), doctored satellite photos, and video misrepresented by CNN are sufficient evidence to condemn the citizens of Yugoslavia to death, disability, and poverty by merciless bombing.

At least now the ground rules of the new "humanitarian" style of war are clear.

But one thing. Don't you usually start hanging the "criminals" after the trial? Not 60+ days before the indictment of their leader.

Anyway, here's something you're not likely to see in the US press: an unedited interview with the "villain du jour," Slobodan Milosevic.

It's from UPI, United Press International, a major press service that is a competitor of the AP. How this managed to get buried by newsrooms across the country is one of the many mysteries of US journalism.

Obviously, like all people who've attained an elevated position in government, Milosevic's statements are bound to be self-serving, but consider this: The US has been engaged in a non-stop bombing campaign against civilians for 60+ days in order to "get" this guy and yet this is probably the longest, and maybe the only exposure, you've ever been given to his side of the story.

***

BELGRADE, April 30 (UPI) - Here is the transcript of Yugoslav President Slobodan Milosevic's interview Thursday with UPI's Arnaud de Borchgrave:

Q: What do you hope to get out of this?

Milosevic: I find it hard to believe what is happening. America is a great country and Americans are great people. But your leaders are not strategic thinkers. Short-term quick fixes, yes. They said let's bomb Yugoslavia and then figure out what to do next.

Some said Milosevic would give up Kosovo after a few days of aggression from the air. To set out to destroy a country for a pretext no one can buy is simply unbelievable. I don't expect to get anything out of this because I did not start it. You may recall there were no refugees before March 24 when the NATO aggression started. But the Clinton administration did expect to get something out of this terrible decision.

I understand you had two general goals. One dealing with Europe, the other with the Balkans. First is to prove U.S. leadership in Europe and the second to re-establish U.S. leadership in NATO in the post-Cold War era.

Regretfully, we were targeted as a guinea pig to achieve those goals. Simply because of our weaknesses and of the internal problems we faced. But, as you know, you will find in at least 100 countries around the world different ethnic separatist movements.

If you decide to support separatist movements it is very hard to believe any country can survive. There are 4,000 ethnic groups in the world and only 185 members of the United Nations. In Yugoslavia, we have 26 different ethnic groups. Any one of them could cause trouble if agitated from the outside. Which is what happened in Kosovo.

In Belgrade, we have 100,000 Yugoslav Albanians. And never a problem with them. Walk from our Parliament building and you will see many shops with their Albanian names. Not one window smashed here in all those years of violence in Kosovo. Our people never considered them responsible for the behavior of the so-called Kosovo Liberation Army terrorists.

In Kosovo, Albanian Kosovars were bigger victims of the KLA than Kosovar Serbs. When we looked at the figures the number of Albanians killed by them was twice as large as Serbs dead. They simply terrorized Albanians to join their underground and impose their idea of an ethnically pure state. That movement is Nazi in its character because of their publicly declared goals of a racially pure state. Where can you find such a state in the world today? It is precisely the opposite of what is happening in the world. Ethnically mixed states are the trend in the new global village. The Kosovar terrorists were trying to reverse a global phenomenon.

Q: Which you then attempted to do in Kosovo after March 24?

Milosevic: Absolutely not. That is the big lie which, repeated often enough, becomes conventional wisdom.

Q: You are denying that your armed forces drove people out of their homes and torched entire villages?

Milosevic: We are not angels. Nor are we the devils you have made us out to be. Our regular forces are highly disciplined. The paramilitary irregular forces are a different story. Bad things happened, as they did with both sides during the Vietnam war, or any war for that matter.

We have arrested those irregular self-appointed leaders. Some have already been tried and sentenced to 20 years in prison. We reinforced our forces after Rambouillet for a major offensive against KLA terrorists, not to ethnically cleanse Kosovo as was done with the expulsion of 500,000 Serbs from Croatia, which was ignored by the world media. And the refugees were fleeing in panic because of the war against the terrorists and also because of disinformation horror stories being spread by the terrorists which then became word of mouth and forced ever more people to join the exodus.

Q: Satellite recon shows entire villages torched?

Milosevic: Individual houses, yes. But not whole villages as we saw on TV in Vietnam when American forces torched villages suspected of hiding Viet Cong.

Q: Just in the past 10 years, the Soviet Union has become 15 independent republics. Four former republics of Yugoslavia have declared their independence. Scotland and

Wales are moving toward self rule. As we approach the next millennium, it is becoming increasingly obvious that the nation-state is too big for small problems - and too small for big problems. Devolution is going on everywhere. Why not in Kosovo? What is so important there?

Milosevic: To us Kosovo is critically important because it is the heart of the country and an integral part of our long history. It is also home to a quarter of million Serbs whose forebears have lived there for centuries. It is also home to some 5,000 Christian churches. A Swiss expert categorized 1,800 of them as historical monuments that are the heritage of world civilization and that list was sent to President Clinton.

Q: After thousands of NATO strikes against Yugoslavia, most of your country's communications and transportation networks, as well as your petroleum production and storage capacity, have been largely destroyed, along with your principal bridges, or about $100 billion worth of damage and about 1,000 killed. Now NATO is raising the total number of warplanes in action against you from 700 to 1,000. Are you prepared to see Yugoslavia's entire infrastructure destroyed?

Milosevic: We never thought we could defeat NATO, an alliance of some 700 million people armed with the most advanced and sophisticated weaponry in the world. But NATO believes it can pick on a small nation and force us to surrender our independence. And that is where NATO miscalculated.

You are not willing to sacrifice lives to achieve our surrender. But we are willing to die to defend our rights as an independent sovereign nation. The U.S. Congress is beginning to understand that bombing a country into compliance is not a viable policy or strategy.

I think your strategic thinkers are also beginning to understand that missiles and other sophisticated weapons will not always be the monopoly of high-tech societies. And with the example it is now setting, we can see the day when lesser nations will be able to retaliate. The development of these weapons is taking place so fast there is not a single spot on the planet that cannot be reached. America can be reached from this part of the world. We have no quarrel with America. We all know NATO is the strongest military machine in the world. We simply want them to stop being so busy with our country and worry about their own problems. NATO was formed to defend the western democratic nations from totalitarian aggression, not to commit aggression. We just want to be left alone and free.

Q: At the cost of another month of bombing?

Milosevic: Tell me, what choice do we have?

Q: It seems to be that being left alone is not an option in what you called a global village. Doesn't your future lie with the European Union in an increasingly integrated Europe? This will require compromise to end this war. Surely the rest of Europe has a stake in what happens in Yugoslavia. Doesn't the EU have a role to play in this impasse? Isolation is not an answer.

Milosevic: Just the opposite. In fact, our policy has been consistent on this front. We launched a series of initiatives with a view to increasing integration in the Balkans. We had a highly successful conference in Crete a year ago.

I met with the Albanian prime minister in an attempt to normalize relations completely with open borders and freedom of movement, free trade and so forth. My point to him was that borders in Europe were becoming irrelevant and that we could not be holdouts against these trends.

European countries have no other choice than to cooperate and integrate. We had a follow-up conference of all the southeastern European nations in Istanbul. I suggested to Bulgaria we do the same we had already done with Macedonia, namely abolish customs duties and open borders for free trade. The same was offered to Bosnia and all other states in the region. With a very simple idea in mind. We are all market economies now. In fact, Yugoslavia is a little bit ahead in this respect having started before the collapse of the Soviet Union and communism.

I told all my neighbors that we could not afford to wait to enter the EU one by one in the years ahead. We had to do something together as a region which would then facilitate joining the wider European enterprise later but earlier than would otherwise be the case. Parallel with this was the process of privatization which we started long before our former communist neighbors. We privatized our telecommunications 18 months ago with Italian and Greek companies. Telecom Serbia is now 50 percent owned by foreign entities. Up and down the line our policy has been one of integration, not isolation. Your policy has been to isolate us and demonize us and get NATO to treat us as a pariah state.

Q: After you walked away from the Rambouillet accords on Kosovo, did you really expect more than a month of sustained bombing?

Milosevic: Rambouillet was not a negotiation. It was a Clinton administration diktat. It wasn't take it or leave it. Just take it or else. We did not expect bombing. It was unbelievable to us that even as an excuse that we didn't want to sign something that we weren't even negotiating it would be used to bomb us as the Nazis did in World War II.

Rambouillet was a recipe for the independence of Kosovo, which clearly we could not accept. Especially given the fact that we never contemplated depriving Kosovar Albanians of their legitimate rights.

The proof is what happened when half a million Serbs were forced out of Croatia. We never retaliated by expelling a single Croat from Serbia. When Serbs were expelled from Bosnia, we protected all our Muslims from retaliation. We never considered Muslims in Yugoslavia were responsible for what happened in Bosnia. Of course there were irresponsible Serb politicians in Bosnia making all kinds of demagogic threats. But this was heated rhetoric. Foreign visitors are invariably impressed at how we handle our unique minorities problems.

Go to Vojvodina in the north and see how the Hungarian minority of 360,000 is treated - it after Hungary became a member of NATO and has now offered its bases to American warplanes to attack us. They have schooling in their own language, their own newspapers and radio and TV programs. Twenty-six such communities enjoy the same rights. There is no other way in such a diversified society. It has been our philosophy from the very beginning. In Kosovo as well.

Equality was the basic principle in Kosovo. Without equality between the two communities there would be no basis for durable peace. That was our approach for Rambouillet. But the American approach was to favor the Albanian community. This could only lead to ethnic cleansing of anyone who was not of Albanian origin. Serbs clearly could not have stayed under the overlordship of Albanians. There are 250,000 Serbs in Kosovo and 200,000 Muslim Serbs who are not of Albanian origin but whose families converted to Islam under the Ottoman Empire. Then you have 150,000 Gypsies and 50,000 Turks. Even this last community has its own newspaper and TV program. U.S. diplomats knowledgeable about Kosovo have confirmed that we were indeed respecting those principles. So I said to them, "OK, gentlemen, now please put those principles into the Rambouillet agreement." Equality means nothing unless incorporated into the institutions.

Q: And how did you propose to do this in practice?

Milosevic: Very simple. Takes only one minute to explain.

The parliament in Kosovo has to be composed of two houses. The lower house elected on the basis of one-citizen one-vote and the other house to be made up of national communities, with each community entitled to five representatives. That way everyone is guaranteed against majority domination. That way, too, Serbs could not impose anything on Albanians and vice versa.

When I talked to Ibrahim Rugova (the moderate Kosovar Albanian leader), we agreed that it was in our common interest to have real peace, welfare for all citizens, clean towns and villages and develop industry. But at the back of the minds of Kosovar Albanians is how to become the masters of the rest of the population.

Several decades ago when the Albanians had complete power in their hands, they started a process of Albanization of the rest of the population. Gypsies, for example, could not register a newly born child unless willing to give it one of the officially recognized Albanian first names.

In Rambouillet, regardless of the fact that the delegations never met, never exchanged so much as a single word, we had a delegation in which Serbs were a minority. We had three Albanians, Serb Muslims, Turks and four Serb Christians. Our delegation represented a real cross-section of Kosovo. The Albanian Kosovars were all representatives of the Albanian separatist movement.

The EU's dilemma at the end of the 20th century is whether they are going to support a multi-ethnic and multi-cultural society and multi-religious approach to society or a kind of Nazi-like approach with one racially pure ethnic group ruling a diverse society like Kosovo. Henry Kissinger said Rambouillet was a mechanism for permanent creation of problems and confrontation. President Clinton should have listened to this wise geopolitical expert rather than some of his own less knowledgeable advisers.

Q: So how do we get out of this mess?

Milosevic: A political process, not by more bombing.

Q: But you must be prepared to compromise.

Milosevic: From the beginning of April I have had five meetings with Rugova. He was not a prisoner or under duress. This week, the President of Serbia went to Pristina (the capital of Kosovo) and he and Rugova signed a statement of agreed joint principles, which called for respect for the equality of national communities, respect for the equality of all citizens, direct negotiations, because U.S. shuttle diplomacy was completely useless as Rambouillet demonstrated. So we have ourselves begun a real political process. This first joint statement with the Albanian Kosovar leader is the first joint victory in our struggle for peace.

At the same time we have been talking about the formation of a temporary joint executive board for Kosovo composed of representatives of all national communities in Kosovo. Its first task will be to help refugees return home. The problem for returning refugees will be bombing. So clearly this insanity will have to stop. Before bombing, regardless of what you hear from NATO and Pentagon briefings, there were no refugees. It wasn't only the Albanians who fled, but also the Serbs, Turks, everyone.

Q: Are you saying that the idea of a U.S. Trusteeship or protectorate is a non-starter in your mind?

Milosevic: Please tell me why a U.N. protectorate is needed. That is not to say we are against a U.N. mission. Before the war, we accepted 2,000 verifiers from ONCE. It was Oscine's biggest ever mission. We also had in Kosovo the International Red Cross and the United Nations High Commission for Refugees, both with huge missions. Plus 1,000 journalists from all over the world, with no restrictions. Plus Kosovo Observation Diplomatic Mission run by Embassies from Belgrade. All this in Kosovo. So who could say we were not open to the international community?

They were all free to verify what was happening in this small territory. But this was abused.

Q: How?

Milosevic: Foreign diplomatic missions were to all intents and purposes supporting KLA terrorists. Instructing them how to organize and what to do to achieve their objectives. Also to create something that would look more like a regular army. That way they were told to create the kind of situation that would make it look to the rest of the world that there was a war between the regular Yugoslav army and the KLA. The KLA was then composed of different terrorist groups. Just judge them by their acts. They were never able to attack any military or police unit. Instead they were taking hostages and killing civilians. One hundred and fifty hostages were never seen again. They were planting car bombs and dynamiting supermarkets. Classic terrorism.

Q: Are you suggesting that since the U.N. and other international organizations couldn't do anything before, you see no point in bringing them back now?

Milosevic: No, not at all. The U.N. can have a huge mission in Kosovo if it wishes. They can bear witness to the legal behavior of our law enforcement agencies and to the fact that everything is now peaceful, that the KLA has ceased to exist except for scattered small groups that can still stage ambushes.

Q: Is it possible to have a U.N. presence without a U.N. peacekeeping force?

Milosevic: We cannot accept an occupation force, whether it flies under a NATO or U.N. flag.

Q: So you accept a U.N. peacekeeping force?

Milosevic: Yes, but no army.

Q: Without weapons?

Milosevic: Self-defense weapons is normal, but no offensive weapons. We cannot accept anything that looks like an occupation. The idea behind Rambouillet was 28,000 troops, including 4,000 Americans, who would be occupying Kosovo with tanks, APCs and heavy weaponry. Kosovo has social and economic problems which an army of occupation cannot alleviate. Aid, not arms, is what Kosovo needs.

Q: So in your judgment what is the nature of a compromise between NATO and Yugoslavia?

Milosevic: I will tell you. Several points. First of all, cessation of all military activities. Second, simultaneity between the withdrawal of NATO troops now concentrated on our borders in Albania and Macedonia, on the one hand, and the decrease of our own troops in Kosovo from their present level of 100,000 to the normal garrison strength of between 11, 000 and 12,000, which was the regular Pristina Corps.

Q: You went from 40,000 to 100,000 troops in Kosovo since the bombing started?

Milosevic: Yes, because of the danger of aggression across our borders by NATO forces. Every day we heard NATO voices urging political leaders to order ground forces into action. But if the danger of NATO aggression is over, we can send our troops back to Serbia. Some are mobilized reservists and they are anxious to get back to their regular jobs.

Q: How long would such a simultaneous withdrawal take in your judgment?

Milosevic: We can do it in one week.

Q: And the third point?

Milosevic: The return of all refugees, regardless of their ethnic or religious affiliation.

Q: And when would the U.N. peacekeeping force go in? Before the refugees can return presumably.

Milosevic: I don't like the word "force." We would welcome U.N. mission, not what "force" implies. There is no job for forces. What would such forces do? Just ruin our roads with their tracked vehicles. We would welcome anyone, any mission, that accepts to be our guests. Their mission would be to observe that all is peaceful and not to act as an occupation force. They can see that we are not terrorizing anybody. Even now we are not terrorizing anybody. When the U.N. is here they can bear witness that what we are saying is the truth.

Q: I assume you know that NATO will not accept your idea of a compromise.

Milosevic: Well, I don't know what NATO will accept. IF NATO insists on the occupation of our country, we have no choice but to defend ourselves against this further act of aggression.

Q: If you wouldn't quibble about the word "force" for U.N. peacekeepers, the end of hostilities could be speeded up.

Milosevic: But I told you we are willing to accept a U.N. presence and are ready to negotiate its composition. But please understand that after all those crimes against our nation and its people, we cannot accept representatives of the countries that committed aggression against us. We would like to see representatives of neutral countries.

Q: Any further points?

Milosevic: My fourth point is the political process. We will continue direct negotiations with Mr. Rugova in the presence of the international community. They can listen to every single word that is spoken, but they cannot act as mediators. We want to achieve the widest possible autonomy for Kosovo within Serbia. So we must negotiate the composition of new institutions and the local police. Before the war, there were

120 villages with elected Albanian local police. Some were killed by KLA terrorists. My fifth point is free access for UNHCR and the International Red Cross. Sixth, an economic recovery plan for the three Yugoslav federation states that have been heavily damaged by NATO aggression.

Q: Back to the composition of U.N. peacekeepers, which you don't like to call a force. Since NATO members are not acceptable, what would you see to European participation as EU, not as individual NATO countries?

Milosevic: There are European countries that are not members of NATO, like Ireland, that would be acceptable.

Q: Contingents from Russia, Ukraine and Belarus have also been mentioned.

Milosevic: They, too, would be acceptable.

Q: Surely you are not prepared to face several more weeks of NATO bombing as the diplomatic haggling continues.

Milosevic: One more day is too much. But what choice do we have if NATO insists on occupying Yugoslavia. To that we will never surrender. We Serbs are as one on this life and death issue of national honor and sovereignty.

An incident waiting to happen

May 29, 1999

You might have missed this earlier this week:

"LONDON (Reuters) - President Clinton is ready to consider a full-scale Kosovo ground war against Serb forces, sending up to 90,000 U.S. combat troops if no peace deal emerges within three weeks, Britain's Times newspaper reported Thursday."

Or this from today's SF Chronicle:

"Britain's defense minister, George Robertson, indicated his country was prepared to contribute as many as 50,000 British soldiers, the official said."

What Clinton, Clark, Blair, and their handlers want and what the American people will tolerate are two different things. So how will Clinton & Co. "sell" the US public on a full scale ground war? (Remember, this started 60+ days ago as "limited" bombing of military-only targets for "humanitarian" purposes.)

A technicolor incident is needed and since NATO seems intent on its ground war option, the only question now is what form will the incident take.

What follows is NATO's golden opportunity - and the fact that it was publicized by the Associated Press, the prime conduit of NATO propaganda, is significant:

"The International Rescue Committee, a private humanitarian organization based in New York, announced plans Friday to begin airdrops of food and supplies in Kosovo for hundreds of thousands of displaced ethnic Albanians. The first missions, scheduled for Monday, will be flown by Moldovan pilots in private planes..."

So far so good.

"Air Force Maj. Gen. Charles Wald, a Pentagon spokesman and F-16 pilot... said NATO will not patrol the air corridor the humanitarian group uses, meaning the private planes will be defenseless if the Serbs fire on them.

State Department spokesman James P. Rubin said there are plans to inform the Yugoslav military of the humanitarian flight schedule."

Note that Rubin says "there are plans to inform..." By what channel does he intend to reach all the relevant forces in time given the flights are starting *Monday* and NATO is doing everything possible to disrupt Yugoslav military communications?

Can you predict what's coming?

What could be more atrocious than the shooting down of a plane on a humanitarian relief mission? What could be firmer proof of "the evil nature of the Serbs?"

The scene has been set masterfully. NATO is on record as saying the flights are risky and they don't recommend them. Of course, why they can't spare even *one* escort plane to protect the food drops when they have hundreds available to bomb civilian population centers in violation of US law is not even brought up.

And the State Department will be able to say over CNN footage of the burning wreckage: "We informed Milosevic of the flight schedule."

"I think it's not a good idea, frankly, as an airman," said Wald... "One reason I say that is because I have zero trust in what (Yugoslav President Slobodan) Milosevic or his army might try to do."

What might the Yugoslavian military do when, in the middle of a war, they see an unknown plane flying over their territory? Shoot it down, of course. What other option do they have? Are they now to allow every plane that flies over their airspace free access because 60+ days into the war a private group suddenly announces they are going to start an undisclosed number of air drops?

There is, of course, a very simple way to safeguard the food drops, but NATO will never suggest it: Halt all the bombing in Kosovo and elsewhere now.

This way it will be crystal clear to the scattered forces of the Yugoslavian military in Kosovo that the "humanitarian" planes are what they say they are and not more NATO craft sent to kill them.

But clearly, given that NATO cannot even be bothered to protect these flights, NATO's purpose is not relief. Relief of the suffering in Kosovo and elsewhere in Yugoslavia is simply not a NATO goal. The goal is to get its troops in and these ill-advised flights are, potentially, their golden key.

The timing is certainly right. The shooting down of a relief plane would fill the headlines and simultaneously discredit the protestors who will be showing up in droves in Washington and San Francisco a week from today.

"We are not paid to be moral"

May 31, 1999

"Goebbels... was using my book 'Crystallizing Public Opinion' as a basis for his destructive campaign against the Jews... Obviously the attack on the Jews of Germany was no emotional outburst of the Nazis, but a deliberate planned campaign."

- Edward Bernays, US inventor of modern corporate public relations, "The Biography of an Idea: Memoirs of Public Relations Counsel Edward L. Bernays"

***

"We are professionals. We had a job to do and we did it. We are not paid to be moral"

It should be clear to anyone who has done even the slightest research on the subject that there are very, very few true journalists practicing in the world today. Most reporters simply repeat what they are told by authorities and their "investigations" are usually little more than elaborations of the currently fashionable party line.

For those who have tried to battle it, the thick wall of prejudice against the Serbs generated by the mainstream western news media has been all but insurmountable.

No atrocity is considered beyond them and if there is no evidence readily at hand, manufacturing it is considered acceptable. No punishment - ruining their food and water supplies, destroying their hospitals and clinics, murdering their children - is considered too extreme.

One question rarely asked is who starts these fashions? When the fashion is to slander one group to the point of death, answering this question is particularly urgent.

The question of the origin of the current hate speech campaign against the Serbs is answerable. Like many 'crystallized' public opinions, it was engineered by professionals who spend their lives creating images for public consumption. (The book "Toxic Sludge is Good For You" by Stauber and Rampton, Common Courage Press, is an excellent introduction to the mechanics of how the public is "sold" ideas.)

The key procedures usually take place in the office of a US public relations company. Since World War One, there has been a great deal of cooperation between those in public relations (PR), the military, intelligence agencies and US corporations.

Surprisingly, it is not that difficult to discover the seed of a manufactured idea. Public relations executives are, like everyone else, fond of their "accomplishments" and often can be found bragging about them.

In 1993, French TV journalist Jacques Merlino published a book entitled: "Les vérités Yougoslaves ne sont pas toutes bonnes à dire" - "Yugoslav truths are not all good for telling."

Reviews of this book have appeared in:

- A Monthly Jewish Review - Midstream, New York, April 1994 ("Stopping the war in Yugoslavia" Author: Dr. Yohanan Ramati)

- Intelligence Digest, Great Britain, February 4, 1994 ("Manipulating the media")

- Jewish Chronicle, Great Britain, December 10, 1993 ("The secret weapon? PR" Author: Nora Beloff)

In his book, Merlino included an interview with James Harff, director of Global Public Affairs for Ruder & Finn, a top 15 US public relations firm. The interview, which was conducted in October of 1993, follows:

Harrf: For 18 months, we have been working for the Republics of Croatia and Bosnia-Herzegovina, as well as for the opposition in Kosovo. Throughout this period, we had many successes, giving us a formidable international image. We intend to make advantage of this and develop commercial agreements with these countries. Speed is vital, because items favourable to us must be settled in public opinion. The first statement counts. The retractions have no effect.

Question: What are your methods of operation?

Harff: The essential tools in our work are a card file, a computer, and a fax. The card file contains a few hundred names of journalists, politicians, academicians, and representatives of humanitarian organizations. The computer goes through the card files according to correlated subjects, coming up with very effective targets.

The computer is tied into a fax. In this way, we can disseminate information in a few minutes to those we think will react (positively). Our job is to assure that the arguments for our side will be the first to be expressed.

Question: How often do you intervene?

Harff: Quantity is not important. You have to intervene at the right time with the right person...

Question: What achievement were you most proud of?

Harff: To have managed to put Jewish opinion on our (Croatian and Bosnian) side. This was a sensitive matter, as the dossier was dangerous when looked at from this angle. President Tidjman (Croatia) was very careless in his book "Wastelands of Historical Reality." Reading this writings, one could accuse him of anti-semitism.

In Bosnia, the situation was no better: President Izetbegovic strongly supported the creation of a fundamentalist Islamic state in his book "The Islamic Declaration." Besides, the Croatian and Bosnian past was marked by a real and cruel anti-semitism. Tens of thousands of Jews perished in Croatian camps. So there was every reason for intellectuals and Jewish organizations to be hostile towards the Croats and Bosnians. Our challenge was to reverse this attitude. And we succeeded masterfully.

At the beginning of August 1992, New York Newsday came out with the affair of (Serb) concentration camps. We jumped at the opportunity immediately. We outwitted three big Jewish organizations - B'Nai Brith Anti-Defamation League, the Jewish Committee, and the American Jewish Congress. We suggested to them to publish an advertisement in the New York Times and to organize demonstrations outside the U.N.

This was a tremendous coup. When the Jewish organizations entered the game on the side of the Bosnians, we could promptly equate the Serbs with the Nazis in the public mind.

Nobody understood what was happening in Yugoslavia. The great majority of Americans were probably asking themselves in which African country Bosnia was situated. But, by a single move, we were able to present a simple story of good guys and bad guys, which would thereafter play by itself.

We won by targeting the Jewish audience. Almost immediately there was a clear change of language in the press, with the use of words with high emotional content, such as "ethnic cleansing", "concentration camps", etc. which evoked images of Nazi Germany and the gas chambers of Auschwitz. The emotional charge was so powerful that nobody could go against it.

Question: But when you did all of this, you had no proof that what you said was true. You only had the article in Newsday!

(Editor's note: The Newsday article was based on a photo staged by a British 'journalist' and contained a number of extreme falsehoods.)

Harff: Our work is not to verify information. We are not equipped for that. Our work is to accelerate the circulation of information favorable to us, to aim at judiciously chosen targets. We did not confirm the existence of death camps in Bosnia, we just made it known that Newsday affirmed it.

Question: Are you aware that you took on a grave responsibility?

Harff: We are professionals. We had a job to do and we did it. We are not paid to be moral."

One important question not answered by this interview: Who directed Croatian, Bosnian, and Kosovar separatist movements - all of which have the creation of an "ethnically pure" state as one of their core tenets - to hire this obviously capable firm?

"Our work is not to verify information... Our work is to accelerate the circulation of information favorable to us."

And who, exactly, is the destruction of Yugoslavia favorable to?

To quote Noam Chomsky, who provided this analysis years before Yugoslavia was in the news:

"The West has a plan for (Eastern Europe) - they want to turn large parts of it into a new, easily exploitable part of the Third World."

***

A report from San Francisco:

"Today I was part of a group of people that filled the Golden Gate Bridge walkway from end to end as a public demonstration calling on NATO to stop bombing in Yugoslavia.

Early on, I met up with a group of Quakers from Santa Rosa, CA, led by Russ & Mary Jorgensen and followed them. One was an 85-year-old woman using a metal walker. She walked two-thirds of the way across the bridge until the San Francisco-side met up with the people walking from the Marin County side. And then she walked back to San Francisco!

If I hadn't seen her I wouldn't have believed it. People in wheelchairs can rest in the chair, but the bridge has no places to sit at all, so this woman was on her feet pushing the walker for two or three hours...

Several television camera crews were out, but I have no idea how many people it takes to fill the bridge from end to end, holding hands. Only time will tell if the print media will cover this..."

- Roy Birchard

June, 1999

NATO's unreported accomplishments

June 1, 1999

We can rely on the AP, the Washington Post and the New York Times to relay NATO's various claims on its front pages: "The bombing is working," "We have hit very few civilians," "The (bridge, refugee shelter, hospital, TV station etc.) was a legitimate military target."

But who's reporting on the international repercussions of the bombings and the price we'll all have to pay for years and years to come, long after the war is over?

From an article by Tariq Ali entitled "The Fallout in Europe" published by CounterPunch (www.counterpunch.org):

"The Ukraine was the only country in the world to renounce nuclear weapons and unilaterally disarm. A few weeks ago its Parliament voted unanimously to revert to its former nuclear status. The deputies claimed that they had foolishly believed the United States when it had promised a new norm-based and inclusive security system. NATO's war on Yugoslavia had destroyed all their illusions...

On 30 April, a meeting of the National Security Council in Moscow approved the modernisation of all strategic and tactical nuclear warheads. It gave the green light to the development and manufacture of strategic low-yield nuclear missiles capable of pin-point strikes anywhere in the world. Simultaneously the Defense ministry authorized a change in nuclear doctrine. First use is no longer excluded...

In the space of several weeks, Javier Solana and Robin Cook, former members of European Nuclear Disarmament, have re-ignited the nuclear flame."

The status of free speech in the US

June 2, 1999

URGENT ACTION NEEDED: Pentagon march permit denied

From: The International Action Center (www.iacenter.org)

In an outrageous effort to suppress the June 5 anti-war march on the Pentagon, the police authorities have denied a permit to march on the streets to the Pentagon. We are launching a massive political and media campaign to demand the right of the protest to march in the streets of Virginia. We believe the White House and the Pentagon are colluding with local police agencies in this effort.

We are appealing to all those who believe in free speech and especially to those who oppose the war in Yugoslavia to assist us in a phone, fax, and email campaign to protect the first amendment rights of all those who plan to participate in the June 5 march on the Pentagon.

With just three days to go before the June 5 march on the Pentagon, the Arlington County Police have denied the June 5th demonstration the right to march on a small stretch of Virginia roadway between the Vietnam Veterans' Memorial, located in Washington DC, and the Pentagon building, located in Virginia. This is an arbitrary and political decision. It is an outrageous attempt to violate the first amendment right to free speech. It is an attempt to either stop the June 5th March on the Pentagon or to create a chaotic situation at the demonstration. While denying the right of the marchers to the roadways leading to the Pentagon, police authorities are trying to reroute the march into a narrow and dangerous bike trail that at points becomes a single-file line, crossing a major highway. The police know that this is not a safe or tenable route for a march of ten thousand or more. The Arlington County Police refuse to return phone calls from the organizers and attorneys of the June 5 march.

The June 5 demonstration is the largest mobilization to date against the U.S./NATO war in Yugoslavia. We believe that it is impossible for the county of Arlington police to unilaterally try to prevent us from carrying out an orderly demonstration. We hold the Clinton White House and Virginia Governor James Gilmore responsible for this flagrant violation of our rights.

We will not be stopped. The war in Yugoslavia has killed thousands of innocent civilians. We will not allow the U.S. authorities to stop the anti-war movement from exercising its rights.

The back of the bus

June 3, 1999

BULLETIN: The government of Yugoslavia has surrendered and accepted NATO's terms, but that's not good enough for Clinton and Blair.

BELGRADE (Reuters) - Yugoslav President Slobodan Milosevic Thursday accepted an international peace plan for Kosovo but President Clinton vowed NATO bombing would continue until Serbian words were matched by deeds.

***

The back of the bus

The New York Times ran a short item today with the headline "UN Finds Proof of 'Ethnic Cleansing' in Kosovo."

You have to read the article to the very last paragraph to discover that there are other refugees in the Balkans besides ethnic Albanians: 500,000 Serbians who the UN says are living in "subhuman conditions."

These 500,000 were 'cleansed' from their homes four years ago and longer. Jared Israel sums up the story of how half of them were rendered homeless in a matter of days:

"In 1995 the Croatian Army, trained, led and given air support by the Pentagon, launched a blitzkrieg against the Krajina section of Croatia, driving out in a matter of days approximately 250,000 Serbian men, women and children whose ancestors had lived in that mountainous region since medieval times.

Thousands were strafed by U.S. planes or slaughtered by Croatian troops as they fled." Source: www.counterpunch.

Somehow, this US-sponsored action didn't qualify as an atrocity or ethnic cleansing.

***

By the way, who gets the mineral deposits?

The New York Times let another well hidden cat out of the bag today, 70+ days into the war: the mineral wealth of Kosovo. The short article entitled "Issue of Who Control's Kosovo's Rich Mines" brings up - for the first time in the mainstream US press - the fact that Kosovo is rich in mineral wealth.

"Experts say the resources include large deposits of coal, along with some nickel, lead, zinc, and other minerals."

In fact, Kosovo has the *largest* deposits of lead in Europe and the largest deposits of coal in all of southeastern Europe.

I wonder what took the Times so long to mention this little fact?

Now, as a result of the "humanitarian" war, ownership of these important industrial raw materials, valued in the billions, is suddenly up for grabs.

***

As of today, NATO has succeeded in killing over 2,000 civilians in just two months. This is the same total, combatants and non-combatants, who were killed in the civil war in the *twelve* months preceding the bombing.

***

Sam Smith (prorev.com) passed this along. Can't say I'm surprised, but it's shocking nonetheless:

"Rowan Scarborugh and Valerie Richardson in the Washington Times report that today will mark W.J. Clinton's first meeting with the Joint Chiefs of Staff since the war against Yugoslavia began. 'In fact, the president has not met with the full Joint Chiefs in nine months. For the war in Kosovo, Mr. Clinton has relied on advice from his civilian national security team none of whom has military experience and Gen. Henry Shelton, the Joint Chiefs chairman.'"

Waco veteran General Wesley Clark who has been calling for a ground invasion of Yugoslavia and has been the instigator behind things like bombing medical facilities and electric power plants, has been invited NOT to attend.

Earlier this week, the New York Times quoted a top aide to Joint Chiefs chairman Shelton's staff on the subject of Clark's qualifications to run a war: "The Saceur (Clark's command) staff is not a war-fighting staff. It has never fought or planned a war."

Yet Clark was given the equivalent of a blank check to do with Yugoslavia as he pleased by a president so out of it he didn't even bother to consult with the Joint Chiefs before starting the assault.

And every day of bombing is another day the president is in violation of the War Powers Act and the Constitution. But the AP, Times, Washington Post, CNN and all the other news sources most Americans rely on, are silent on this point.

Seven ways to say no to peace

June 3, 1999

The government of Yugoslavia has agreed to NATO's peace terms, but apparently agreement is not enough to stop the carnage. As this evening's AP article ("Clinton Welcomes Kosovo Agreement") informed the world with quotes from seven US officials, the US has more bombing to do.

1. President Clinton: Until Serb forces begin a verifiable withdrawal from Kosovo, we will... continue the military effort that has brought us to this point.

2. Secretary of State Madeleine Albright: The confrontation cannot end until thcsc tcrms arc complied with and implemented.

3. Defense Secretary William Cohen: Until such time as we're satisfied that they intend to fully comply with the agreement, then the air campaign will continue.

4. State Department spokesman James P. Rubin: We need to codify this and have it implemented for it to be meaningful.

5. Presidential spokesman Joe Lockhart: We're dealing with someone who has made promises before and has not kept them. It is prudent to be cautious.

6. Pentagon spokesman Kenneth Bacon: We have to see performance, not promises.

7. Air Force Maj. Gen. Charles Wald: Until there's agreement, they're a military target.

Seven reasons to protest on June 5

June 4, 1999

1. Before the bombing, Yugoslavia had agreed to peace terms in Kosovo, but would not agree to NATO's demand that NATO troops be allowed to occupy the entire country.

2. The US and NATO were aware that the bombing would worsen the refugee situation, but proceeded with it anyway and failed to make adequate preparations for the refugees.

3. Civilian installations (hospitals, bridges, television stations, schools, food processing plants, electrical power plants) were classified as legitimate military targets and bombed.

Over 2,000 civilians have been killed by NATO bombing to date. (First brasscheck report on civilian casualties: March 30)

4. As of May 26, all US involvement in this war was in violation of the War Powers Act and the Constitution of the United States. Source: Washington Post (Original source no longer available.)

5. The bombing has re-ignited the nuclear arms race and created distrust for the US around the world.

6. The bombing is being paid for with the US Social Security fund and is eliminating the US budget surplus.

7. The bombing continues today even though the Yugoslavian Parliment has agreed to the peace terms.

March on June 5, 1999

In Washington: Starts at 12 noon at the Vietnam Veterans Memorial and marches to the Pentagon. (Due to overwhelming public pressure, the march's permit was approved after initially being rejected.)

In San Francisco: Gather, 11 a.m. UN Plaza, Market St., between 7th & 8th Sts. March, 12 noon to Dolores Park, 18th & Dolores St. for rally beginning at 1 p.m.

***

The latest news:

"Clark said NATO troops, working with international relief workers, will try to persuade refugees in camps in Macedonia and Albania to delay returning to Kosovo. But 'this may not be possible,' the general acknowledged. 'This is going to be a tough, difficult, dirty job.'"

Source: "Troops Are Ready To Enter Kosovo" Washington Post 6/4/99

"Raytheon Co. expects to receive about $1 billion in orders to replenish stocks of cruise missiles and other weapons fired during the air war against Serbia, the company's chief executive said yesterday."

Source: The Boston Globe 6/4/99

In case you thought the war was over

June 8, 1999

"I don't see any difference in the behavior of NATO and of Hitler. NATO wants to erect its own order in the world, and it needs Yugoslavia simply as an example: 'We'll punish Yugoslavia, and the whole rest of the planet will tremble."

- Alexander Solzhenitsyn (Quoted by counterpunch.com)

***

BRUSSELS, June 7 (AFP) - NATO said Monday it had resumed bombing of Yugoslavia at intense levels after the break down of talks on a Serb withdrawal from Kosovo.

"Operations on Day 76 (of the air campaign) are underway and accelerating towards their prior intensity," the alliance said in a statement.

"To sum it up: The NATO generals announced that they changed their mind about everything. There'll be no UN overseeing the occupation. Instead of the UN presence, NATO will be the supreme decision maker, with only the NATO troops handling everything. The shell game is complete. No one here is surprised at all, although there are plenty disappointed. I guess we all keep being naive, despite all the evidence."

***

The New York Times marches on

"Now, onward to the next Kosovo. If there is one." - Headline across the top of the front page of the Week in Review section

"After victory, it's tempting to think about making a habit of bombing for peace" - Subhead from same article

Take out the qualifiers, "if there is one" and "it's tempting to think..." and you have rhetoric comparable to what appeared in the newspapers of the Third Reich. The important difference being during the Third Reich statements like these came from a depraved madman with dictatorial power over the press. In the US, the press *volunteers* them under the guise of "critical analysis."

If the Times reported on the peace demonstrations in San Francisco, Washington DC, and elsewhere they hid it pretty well. I couldn't find a mention of them, nor of the fact there is a large and active worldwide anti-war movement opposing the bombings that includes the governments of many nations.

Sam Smith sends this along from Greece's Council of State, the highest administrative court in that country:

"NATO's offensive against a sovereign European state, unprecedented in the post-war years, is an affront not only to the ethical principles of Greek and European civilisation, but also to the fundamental precepts of international law. This latter is a legal issue and should not be overshadowed by the moral revulsion that is justly provoked by this cowardly and barbaric attack."

The US news media in the war's service

June 8, 1999

"The targets in the assault on Yugoslavia appear to be similar to those singled out during the assaults on Iraq in the 1990s and Nicaragua in the 1980s (not to mention the mini-assault on Sudan last year): basic economic and social service infrastructure." - Brasscheck, March 30, 1999

***

The US media in the war's service

Is it news or propaganda? - Episode 273

FAIR (Fairness and Accuracy in Reporting) did an online search of the major US news outlets including the New York Times, the Washington Post, CNN, ABC, NBC, CBS, and PBS's NewsHour, to look for reporting on last Saturday's peace marches in Washington DC, San Francisco, and elsewhere.

The results? Zero. No reports, not even a passing mention.

How many readers remember the multi-day coverage of a very minor protest in Belgrade that took place a few weeks ago? A few hundred people there protested conscription. If I recall correctly, that story made the AP.

I guess in the case of the New York Times, its editors were too busy Saturday crafting headlines like: "Now, onward to the next Kosovo." (See "Week in Review" June 6, 1999.)

Anyone surprised by this should review the record of the major US news media during the 1930s. They lionized Mussolini and news services like Hearst's were actually in the employ of the Nazi government. This episode was best documented by George Seldes in "Even the Gods Can't Change History." Seldes was publisher of "In fact" and authored numerous books on the US news media. The mention of his name was officially banned from the New York Times for several decades as the result of his pointed, and accurate, criticism of that paper. (www.brasscheck.com/seldes)

***

Fortunately, not all US media outlets are dispensing propaganda...

More valuable contributions from CounterPunch:

1. The complete text of Regis Debray's letter to French President Chirac on his seven day tour of Kosovo in early May.

The existence of this letter and reference to its contents was mentioned briefly by Reuters (by its entertainment bureau!) about a month ago. That story was followed up by news wire accounts documenting attacks on Debray, declaring that his act of bearing witness to the events in Kosovo was the equivalent of "intellectual suicide."

2. "The Twilight of the European Project: by Peter Gowan currently in the CounterPunch home page. This essay is among the best accounts of how the war came about and why.

Lest we forget what this is all about, a current accounting of the number of civilians - men, women, boys and girls - killed and injured by the daily NATO bombings. Includes the cities, towns, and villages targeted and the weapons used: www.counterpunch.org/dead.html (Original source no longer available.)

Micro-censorship: The news from San Francisco

June 8, 1999

Earlier today, I reported that Saturday's peace marches were completely blacked out by all major US news media outlets. "But what about local reporting?" some asked. Surely the local news can't ignore thousands of people marching in the streets, can it?

Read on for a lesson in US news control...

This report comes from Silvia the San Francisco woman who runs www.keepfaith.com. The site features daily reports from Belgrade filed by her mother, 74 year old retired journalist Ivanka Besevic.

In this report, Silvia reports on how the local San Francisco press covered the peace march there. A person I know who was there and has long experience counting crowds guessed "at least 5,000" which, given that so many people had been duped into believing the bombing was over, was a pretty healthy turnout.

Here's how the local news reported it:

“COVERAGE

* The San Francisco Chronicle wrote there were "over a thousand" marchers - another fine example of telling the truth while twisting it just a bit. I can say that Chronicle sells over 100 copies a day, and be right too...

* Channel 7 did after all cover the demonstration, during the 11pm news, in a short but objective blurb.

* Channel 4 had no mention of it. (Note: The Chronicle owns the station.)

* Channel 2 was AMAZING! It had an extensive and what I can only consider deliberately slanted coverage. Only a couple of demonstrators were interviewed, all Serb/American, after which there was mention of the buses that brought people in, creating the impression that the bus loads of Serbs were brought in to demonstrate and they were the only ones (the Serb contingent was a minuscule part).

Then, after a short shot of the demonstration itself, there was a longer segment interviewing people on the streets. Four out of the five interviewed were strongly pro bombing, and the last one held a speech about the refugees from Kosovo. As I was there and had talked to people watching, I know for the fact that it took a concerted effort to find only the people who were pro-aggression on the Balkans. Most of the onlookers were against it, and honked, yelled and waved to show it.

The segment closed with the menacing mention of the strong police presence, "but no arrests were made." Were they taping the same demonstration??? This last one was completely inaccurate - the demonstration of about a month ago that had only 1,500 people had a double or triple police presence! As I said earlier, I suspect that the police didn't expect the impressive turnout after the signing of the capitulation, and had only the minimum numbers of police - there were some cops on the motorcycles, between us and traffic, and only one police van that I noticed at all. The demonstration of a month ago had three police vans. An excellent example of creative editing..."

(Note: Channel 2 often coordinates closely with the Examiner. Still owned by the patriotic Hearst family which never saw an American war they didn't like. Managing editor Sharon Rosenhause proposed stripping Gary Webb of a local journalism award given to him for his Contra-Cocaine connection articles. She coordinated her smear of Webb so closely with her colleagues at the New York Times that her proposal was page two news the very day she made it!)

***

George Seldes wrote a colorful piece on the conduct of the San Francisco press during the 1934 General Strike. Even Seldes, who had seen it all, was amazed at the duplicity of the city's papers.

Seldes' report along with Silvia's should give anyone who has had the experience of watching the performance of San Francisco's uniquely dishonest newspapers a strong sense of deja vu. (www.brasscheck.com/1934.html)

Is NATO bombing withdrawing Yugoslavian troops?

June 9, 1999

Q: Who said the following on March 27 before ordering a massive air assault on Belgrade - in the name of international peace and stability?

"I have done everything honestly to bring Yugoslavia into our community (of nations)... Unfortunately these endeavors did not meet with success... Therefore I have...arranged for all necessary measures... with military means."

Answer at the end of this piece

***

Is NATO bombing withdrawing Yugoslav troops?

One of the lasting images of the Iraq War was the unwarranted slaughter of thousands of retreating Iraqi soldiers by air bombardment on the highway leaving Kuwait.

Today, in the midst of peace talks and formal NATO/ Yugoslav coordination on the details of how the Yugoslavian armed forces will leave Kosovo, NATO announced its first successful significant use of air power against a *military* target in Kosovo in over 34,000 missions.

Here's the line from the Washington Post as relayed by the San Francisco Chronicle:

"Several hundred Yugoslav soldiers are believed to have been killed in a raid by an American B-52 bomber that caught them massing in a field near the Kosovo-Albanian border on Monday, NATO sources said yesterday."

"The casualty toll may have been the highest suffered by the Yugoslavs in a single attack since NATO's air war began 11 weeks ago."

The question is why, after 11 weeks of easily evading NATO bombardment, would the battle-tested Yugoslav forces suddenly start massing in the open air in a field in plain sight of NATO bombers?

The Post article offers this:

"NATO military sources said two Yugoslav Army battalions were spotted by allied reconnaissance assembling on a hillside in the Mount Pastrik area. The troops were apparently trying to thwart ethnic Albanian guerrillas who in the past two weeks have mounted an offensive seeking to establish new corridors to the Pec-Prizren road from their border strongholds."

An elaborately detailed, plausible-sounding answer that upon examination raises more questions than it answers.

The war in Kosovo is a guerilla war. The KLA - if it is acting independently without the help of US and UK Special Forces - has the ability to do little more than take random pot shots and lob artillery shells here and there hoping to hit something. (As was demonstrated in the Bosnian and Croatian wars, the only thing US/NATO surrogates can do with any proficiency is kill large numbers of unarmed civilians.)

Why then would the Yugoslavian army suddenly change its successful tactics, abandon its training and experience and respond to the KLA's method of warfare by massing 18th century style in a field?

The Post article offers this non-explanation:

"The recent offensive by ethnic Albanian rebels of the Kosovo Liberation Army has succeeded in flushing out many Yugoslav soldiers who were previously well dispersed and hidden in ways that had made it difficult for NATO warplanes to strike them."

The military coordination of the terrorist KLA and NATO is an open secret that is now apparently suitable for public consumption as the above remark indicates, but this statement confuses the matter even further.

Were these two battalions flushed out by KLA attacks, or were they massing in the open air - against all common sense - for an attack on the KLA? It's got to be one or the other, and neither makes sense.

Here's a possible key: "NATO military sources said... the troops were apparently trying to thwart ethnic Albanian guerrillas..." and so on.

The reliability of NATO accounts has already been demonstrated, so it's fair to hold, as a possibility at least, that NATO is again, with the help of its friends at the Washington Post, lying.

Yugoslavia has been silent about this bombing which took place Monday. Given that there is a war going on, their silence on the matter is understandable. You don't admit or publicize military casualties especially if they are severe.

But what were these two battalions doing, out like sitting ducks in the open air, if not preparing to move in a "verifiable" way out of the area? That's a more plausible explanation than the ones offered by the Post and NATO. If that's the case, the bombing of several hundred soldiers in the process of withdrawing would be in keeping with NATO's consistent multi-year strategy of doing everything possible to undermine peace in the region.

40,000 soldiers have to move out of Kosovo with US-supported KLA terrorists on the ground and NATO bombers in the air. And NATO says it won't stop the bombing until it is satisfied with the withdrawl. Does anyone else see the bind here?

***

Who said this on March 27 before starting the bombing of Belgrade?

"I have done everything honestly to bring Yugoslavia into our community (of nations)... Unfortunately these endeavors did not meet with success... Therefore I have... arranged for all necessary measures... with military means."

Not Bill Clinton.

Adolph Hitler in a wire to Mussolini before beginning the air assault on Belgrade - March 27, 1941. Source: William L. Shirer: "The Rise and Fall of the Third Reich" pages 825, 826.

"Belgrade itself, as Hitler ordered, was razed to the ground. For three days and nights Goering's bombers ranged over the little capital at rooftop level - for the city had no anti-aircraft guns - killing 17,000 civilians, wounding many more and reducing the place to a mass of smoldering rubble. 'Operation Punishment,' Hitler called it."

Ibid p. 826.

Bombing "suspended" - and now, the future

June 10, 1999

"BRUSSELS, Belgium (AP) -- NATO Thursday announced a suspension of its airstrikes against Yugoslavia after verifying the withdrawal of Serb forces was underway."

It appears that NATO has given up on its original goal of the equivalent of a complete military occupation of the entire country of Yugoslavia. However...

"...the U.S. was compelled to sign after the failure of the... bombings... the White House at once announced quite lucidly that they would violate every significant element of the Treaty they were signing (and presented) a different version (of the agreement) which was adopted in reporting and commentary, so that when North Vietnam finally responded to serious U.S. violations of the accords, it became the incorrigible aggressor which had to be punished once again, as it was." Vietnam 1973

Source: Z MAGAZINE: "Kosovo Peace Accord, Analysis by Noam Chomsky"

Ramsey Clark calls for the disbanding of NATO, a quixotic sounding quest if ever there was one. But what is the alternative? Armed forces are, when stripped of all the gloss, killing machines. Nothing more, nothing less. Unfortunately, the *only* way to keep these machines well oiled is to use them, so they are used at regular intervals - against someone. Why, 10 years after the collapse of the Soviet Union, is NATO still in business anyway?

***

"NATO: An organization imposed on the Atlantic Alliance which is no more and no less than the military and political subordination of Western Europe to the United States of America."

- Charles de Gaulle

***

For whom the bell tolls

And for Americans who think this problem is "overseas," 'ask not for whom the bell tolls...'

In "Report on the Americas", May/June 1999, published by North American Congress on Latin America, there is a News Brief reminding us that Pres. Clinton wants to radically change the relationship of the US military to domestic affairs.

"In a January 1999 interview that drew little public attention, President Clinton stated that, as part of a major buildup in counterterror defenses, he was considering a Pentagon proposal to establish a commander for the defense of the continental United States...

The national security establishment sees a range of potential threats, from terrorist assaults on infrastructure or national computer systems to chemical or biological attacks, which, they maintain, law enforcement and civilian agencies are ill-equipped to handle. Military units are required, in this view, to conduct rescue operations, maintain order and defend against terrorist threats.

Role expansion in general and counterterror operations in particular, which draw on counterinsurgency doctrine, tend to politicize militaries. Historically - and certainly in Latin America - large and politicized militaries with domestic security functions have endangered democratic processes.

Distinctions between foreign and domestic enemies become hazy and citizens become suspect. 'Homeland defense' blurs the line between civilian and military authority and gives military commanders increasing influence in political affairs and national decision making. Military units may become a more intrusive presence in society. Domestic military intelligence and surveillance pose threats to freedoms of the press, of assembly, of free speech and expression, and of protection from unreasonable search and seizure. But the US public seems unaware of the recent steps expanding the military's domestic role." - end of quote.

I repeat:

"Armed forces are, when stripped of all the gloss, killing machines. Nothing more, nothing less. Unfortunately, the *only* way to keep these machines well oiled is to use them, so they are used at regular intervals - against someone."

The day the US installs a "a commander for the defense of the continental United States," it will only be a matter of time before US citizens on US soil become *direct* victims of what has been going on, in our names and with our tax dollars, around the world. If you haven't already, see William Bloom's "Killing Hope: U. S. Military and CIA Interventions Since World War II" for what is, potentially, in store for citizens of the United States.

NATO Commander Wesley Clark, now so busy in Yugoslavia, was commander of the Ft. Hood tanks used for the Waco assault. Before that, he was in charge of anticipating new training needs for the "soldier of the 21st century." Apparently, directing the US military to "accidentally" kill innocent people is his highly rewarded contribution to military science.

Given the "success" of his operation against Yugoslavia, Clark is a likely choice to become the first commander for the defense of the continental United States, if and when that position is created.

Like I said: Ask not for whom the bell tolls...

Farce follows tragedy

June 11, 1999

General Wesley Clark - mass murderer (Waco), war criminal (Yugoslavia), Rhodes scholar and Arkansas native - changed the Kosovo deployment plans at the last minute to make sure US troops got there first for the television cameras. While Clark diddled, Yugoslavian ally Russia stole a march on NATO troops and is now in the process of securing territory to protect Serbian civilians against what happened to them the last time NATO "protected" them after a US engineered takeover.

The Russian army is probably the only thing preventing another NATO supported mass dislocation and slaughter of Serbian civilians, such as the one that occured in Croatia earlier in this decade.

There are still 500,000 Serbian refugees from the US adventure in Croatia. Those are the lucky ones the CIA/ Pentagon-coached Croatian military didn't slaughter.

Here's the latest news straight from the wire services. No time for a Pentagon spin. For once, some fairly straight reporting on the situation as it unfolds. It should be an interesting weekend.

British troops' entry into Kosovo delayed by US

LONDON, June 11 (AFP) - The entry of British troops into Kosovo at the head of the NATO-led peacekeeping force was delayed at Washington's insistence, to allow US troops to go in first, British media reports said Friday.

British paratroopers and Gurhkas were ready to move across the Macedonian border at dawn on Friday, but were ordered to stand down only a few hours before, as an order came from Washington putting the operation on hold for 24 hours, it was reported.

Sky Television's correspondent on the Macedonian border said that there was "considerable anger among British officers" at what was seen as an attempt by the United States to claim the glory of being the first to enter Kosovo.

On Friday, the situation suddenly changed as the unexpected push by Russian peacekeepers into Serbia towards Kosovo prompted British troops to begin moving towards the Kosovo border.

According to a journalist from the Daily Mail, providing pool copy for the British media, the United States had demanded the delay to allow them to fly in 2,000 Marines by helicopter from US warships in the Adriatic.

The original order of march called for the British, supported by the Germans and the French on the flanks, to push north from Macedonia through the mountain passes and secure the high plateau beyond.

But under a new plan, US troops were also to be rushed to Gnjilane in eastern Kosovo, with arrangements to ensure that "all the American television networks will be there to record this glorious victory for America's fighting spirit," the Daily Mail correspondent said.

Another correspondent, from the London Evening Standard, said the British and French felt that Washington had tried to turn the KFOR operation "into an American media circus."

Editor's note: No honor among thieves, I guess.

***

MEANWHILE, while General Clark waits for the television cameras to get set up, Russian troops leave US troops flat footed.

RUSSIA, NATO ADVANCE IN RACE TOWARD KOSOVO

By Deborah Charles

BELGRADE (Reuters) - NATO and Russian forces swept toward Kosovo Friday in a race to enter the ravaged province as Serbian troops retreated.

Russian peacekeepers crossed the border from Bosnia into Yugoslavia and headed toward Kosovo in a move that caught the West by surprise.

NATO sources said the alliance had begun its own deployment to Kosovo but could not immediately say if its troops had already entered.

“A few hours ago they were on their way to the border,” a NATO source told Reuters.

Some 50 Russian vehicles, including 20 to 30 armoured personnel carriers, crossed into Serbia from Bosnia and by early afternoon had passed Belgrade en route for Kosovo. The United States said Moscow had given assurances that the troops would not enter the Serbian province unilaterally.

NATO said it was seeking to find out what orders the troops had been given. “Their future intentions are not clear to us,” an alliance source told Reuters.

The surprise Russian move came against a background of stalled negotiations over Moscow's role in an international peacekeeping force to enable the return of hundreds of thousands of ethnic Albanian refugees.

A Russian general said Moscow wanted control over Serb-populated parts of northern Kosovo, with or without NATO's blessing.

“We will not beg, give us this little piece,” General Leonid Ivashov said, adding that Moscow was prepared to negotiate its own sector directly with Belgrade if necessary.

From Waco to Belgrade: Wesley Clark and America's "Army of the Future"

June 14, 1999

Special Brasscheck Report

DID THE TACTICS OF NATO'S COMMANDER WESLEY CLARK IN THE WAR AGAINST YUGOSLAVIA SEEM ODDLY FAMILIAR? THERE'S A GOOD REASON FOR THAT

From Waco To Belgrade: Wesley K. Clark and America's "Army of the Future"

By Ken McCarthy - Brasscheck

www.brasscheck.com/clarkatwaco.html

***

"I knew we would win it. I knew you would win it, Mr. President."

- Gen. Wesley Clark, NATO Supreme Commander to Bill Clinton, fellow 50-something Rhodes Scholar and Arkansan, after NATO agreed to stop bombing Yugoslavia. (Source: "Clinton Claims Victory in Air War" - Terence Hunt, AP White House Correspondent, June 10, 1999)

***

General Wesley Clark was involved in the siege and final assault near Waco, Texas that killed, by a combination of toxic gas and fire, at least 82 people - including some three dozen women, children and infants.

As outlandish as this claim may seem, it's a reasonable conclusion that can be drawn by any fair-minded person who takes the time to examine the evidence. Further, there is substantial circumstantial evidence that Clark, in addition to acting as a tactical consultant, may, in fact, have been the prime architect and commander of the entire operation.

If this is true, why is it important?

First, it represents a clear violation of US law. The military is banned from involvement in the enforcement of US civil law except under certain carefully defined circumstances. The incident at Waco did not come even close to legally qualifying.

Second, it casts light on some of the more outrageous tactics used in the war against Yugoslavia, in particular the bombing attacks on Yugoslavian news media, essential life support services, and on civilians - the latter which were sometimes, but not always, described as "accidents."

Third, President Clinton began the year with the statement that he is considering a Pentagon proposal to create a new US military command, commander-in-chief for the defense of the continental U.S., a first in peace time and an alarming move (for reasons described in "Bombing 'suspended' - and now, the future" www.brasscheck.com/yugoslavia/directory/61099a.html).

One of the officers most likely to receive this appointment would be, as the result of his "success" in Yugoslavia, General Wesley K. Clark.

Fourth, US military leadership must be well aware of Clark's role in Waco, yet they have rewarded him with significant promotions ever since.

* The US military was at Waco

The initial reaction of virtually every person who hears about Clark's involvement in the attack on the Mt. Carmel Center of the Branch Davidians outside of Waco, Texas is surprise and/or disbelief: "I thought it was an ATF/FBI operation that went wrong, and all the military did was lend a few tanks."

Let's start by dispelling that myth. Here is the list of US military personnel and equipment that the US Justice Department admits were used at Mt. Carmel:

"Military Personnel and Equipment

-- Personnel:

Active Duty Personnel - 15

Texas National Guard Personnel - 13

-- Track vehicles:

Bradley fighting vehicle (OMZ) - 9

Combat Engineer Vehicle (M728) - 5

Tank Retrieval vehicle (M88) - 1

Abrams Tanks (M1A1) - 2"

Source: Department of the Treasury, Report of the Department of the Treasury on the Bureau of Alcohol, Tobacco, and Firearms Investigation of Vernon Wayne Howell, also known as David Koresh, U.S. Government Printing Office, September 1993.

The Justice Department list has some very important deliberate omissions as will become clear later in the section on the final assault.

* The real command structure at Waco

Since the recent bombing campaign against Yugoslavia started, "NATO commanders" (i.e. General Wesley Clark) have insisted that NATO, not the UN, would be the commanding force in Kosovo and everyone else, like the Russians, would have to submit to NATO orders. Epic ineptitude on Clark's part may have thwarted NATO's designs, but the lesson is of critical importance for understanding Waco.

It is this: No military commander "lends" 17 pieces of armor and 15 active service personnel under his command to anybody, let alone the FBI or any other law enforcement agency, willingly. The principle is very simple: my men, my arms, my show.

In a lawful operation, the command structure would have been publicly announced, but since the involvement of the military in Waco was entirely illegal and indefensible, it was necessary to paint the situation as an FBI operation. The obviously substantial presence of US military equipment used in the operation was dismissed as being equivalent to a "rent a car" service.

The US news media, which received all of its information on Waco by dutifully attending FBI press conference briefings and then repeating them uncritically, swallowed the "FBI in charge" story hook, line, and sinker.

Still not convinced Waco was a military operation?

There's more.

* The key role of the Fort Hood, Texas army base

The military equipment and personnel used at Waco came from the US Army base at Ft. Hood, Texas, headquarters of III Corps.

Here's a succinct account of the initial raid that caused the standoff, submitted by David T. Hardy, an attorney who battled to force the government to release evidence in the case.

(Take special note of the passages I've marked with *)

"The incident originated in an attempt by the Bureau of Alcohol, Tobacco and Firearms to serve search and arrest warrants on a building, known to its residents as Mount Carmel, located in a rural area a few miles outside of Waco, Texas. The operation required mustering approximately a hundred agents (flown in from sites around the country), and who **received military training** at Ft. Hood. They traveled in a convoy of sixty vehicles and were supported by three National Guard helicopters and one fixed-wing aircraft, **with armored vehicles in reserve.**"

The personnel, described as ATF employees, received military training at Ft. Hood in preparation for the raid. Why?

The reason is that the original charges against the Branch Davidians included drug violations. On the strength of these charges - which later were found to be absolutely false - the ATF qualified to receive military training and other assistance for the raid.

Given that the training was customized for this particular raid, the assistance in all likelihood included intelligence support. In other words, military personnel looked the compound over, drew up attack plans, created a training program for the ATF agents, and then, one would assume, were there on the day of the raid - along with the local news cameras which had been tipped off in advance - to watch the thing go down. (The Department of Justice reports that the code word used to launch the raid was "Showtime.")

Note too that armored vehicles were held "in reserve" on the day of the raid as well. There are at least two published local press photographs that show armored military vehicles at and on their way to the Mt. Carmel center on the very day of the raid. You can see them here:

www.brasscheck.com/yugoslavia/mil1.jpg

www.brasscheck.com/yugoslavia/mil2.jpg

There is another press photograph, taken the day after the raid, which shows at least nine military vehicles stationed at nearby Texas State Technical College, which very soon after the raid, was completely taken over as a command center.

www.brasscheck.com/yugoslavia/mil3.jpg

The presence of so much military-owned equipment on the scene, along with the documented fact that the raid was prepared for at Ft. Hood by military trainers, seems to me to be all the evidence needed to show heavy military involvement preceding the initial raid.

Perhaps equally significant is the amount of dissembling that surrounded the undeniable fact of pre-raid military involvement. For example, the governor of Texas claimed to the press that she requested National Guard presence after the raid.

President Clinton was quoted as saying:

"The first thing I did after the ATF agents were killed, once we knew that the FBI was going to go in, was to ask that the military be consulted because of the quasi-military nature of the conflict." (Washington Times, April 24, 1993)

Attorney General Janet Reno attempted to explain away the "FBI" use of US Army tanks as being equivalent to an innocuous "rent a car" arrangement.

The statements of these three individuals obscure the simple fact that the military vehicles, and personnel who operated and maintained them, were part of the initial raid - and therefore in clear violation of US law.

Also, government statements relayed to the public by the US news media made much of the fact that one of the tanks was operated by an FBI agent. It's interesting to note that no reference was ever made to the operators of the other 16 military vehicles used in the operation.

* Showtime

As I mentioned earlier, the code word that launched the raid was "showtime." The name of the operation itself, according to the aforementioned Department of Justice report, was "Operation Trojan Horse."

Early in the siege, "Operation Trojan Horse" became a popular destination for special forces officers both from around the United States and from its closest ally, the UK. They came to observe the effectiveness of various high tech devices and tactics that were being tested against the Branch Davidians.

Source: London Sunday Times, March 21, 1993: "FBI brings out secret electronic weapons as Waco Siege drags on."

The raid was on February 28. The London Times article ran on March 21. It's noteworthy that Waco became a focus for US and UK special forces officers so quickly. The 3/21

London Times report states that "observer teams from the American Delta Force and British SAS have *already* visited Waco." (Emphasis mine.)

Organizing groups of officers to make a field trip normally takes far more lead time than a couple of weeks. This is the military, not a group of freewheeling bohemians who can pile in a van and travel across the country, or the globe, on a whim. Yet, there they were, with plane and hotel reservations, briefings, tours and the like, all arranged. Such organization implies pre-planning or at least very strong pre-existing relationships with Delta Force and SAS on the part of the officer in charge. It would have taken an officer with unusual connections and motivations to pull off this level of "show and tell."

By the way, the notion that Delta Force and SAS officers would make such a trip to observe the *FBI* using various secret high tech warfare devices is laughable. Who in the FBI would know how to operate them? In any event, the equipment and tactics used came from the military, not any law enforcement agency.

In reality, the FBI was not in charge of the Waco siege. Its role instead was twofold: 1) to keep up fruitless negotiations with the Branch Davidians and 2) to act as the front for the real operation, which was under military command and therefore entirely illegal.

* Cold blooded murder

Based on the claim that Branch Davidian leader David Koresh was abusing the children in the compound - a lie according to survivors - and sympathy for the "tired" FBI agents, Attorney General Janet Reno signed off on the plan for the final assault which resulted in the death by toxic gas and fire of over 80 civilians. Who presented the plan to her?

An article in CounterPunch relates the essential facts:

"Two senior Army officers subsequently traveled to a crucial April 14 meeting in Washington, D.C. with Attorney General Janet Reno and Justice Department and FBI officials in which the impending April 19 attack on the compound was reviewed. The 186-page "Investigation into the Activities of Federal Law Enforcement Agencies Towards the Branch Davidians," prepared by the Committee on Government Reform and Oversight and lodged in 1996 (CR 104 749) does not name these two officers..."

Source: www.counterpunch.org/waco.html (Original source no longer available.)

From the sound of this, it appears clear that the final solution to the growing political problem of Waco came directly from the US military. How odd if, in fact, Waco was an FBI operation.

* The final solution

The final assault on the Mt. Carmel complex occurred in three stages: 1) armored military vehicles punched holes in both ends of the main building of the complex, 2) "crowd control" gas was sprayed in, and 3) a fire started which destroyed the complex.

Witnesses expected that the gas would drive the inhabitants out. Instead, no one came out and the complex was engulfed in fire.

Why didn't the residents come out? The cover story as related by the FBI and the Department of Justice is that the Branch Davidians killed their own children and then themselves, and simultaneously set the complex on fire rather than surrender. There is no forensic evidence to support this claim.

Here's what a Failure Analysis Associates' study found about the nature of the "crowd control" gas that was used:

"1. The first assault started at approximately 6:00 A.M.

CS concentrations in the rooms directly injected by the M5 delivery alone ranged from 2 to 90 times that required to deter trained soldiers.

Methylene chloride concentrations in the rooms directly injected by gas were as high as 1.8 times the IDLH (Immediately Dangerous to Life and Health) concentration and nearly to the concentration that would render a person unconscious.

2. The second assault started at approximately 7:30 A.M.

CS concentrations in the rooms directly injected by gas from M5 delivery alone ranged from 2 to 80 times that required to deter trained soldiers.

Methylene chloride concentrations... were as high as 1.6 times the IDLH..."

All in all, nearly 400 gas-filled projectiles were fired into the building, and CS was sprayed from four tank rack dispensers on the armored vehicles. As Failure Analysis Associates concluded in its report, this was the most intensive use of crowd control chemicals in the history of the United States.

Methylene chloride is even more dangerous than CS - and five pounds of MeCl were injected for every ounce of CS. MeCl is an industrial solvent, with powerful anesthetic properties.

It was once used as paint remover before being banned for that purpose for being too dangerous to handle. Both gasses are flammable.

In other words, the gases used and the quantities they were used in were sufficient to kill many of the inhabitants on contact, especially the young children, and would have been more or less capable of instantly incapacitating the rest.

Finally, there is the issue of the fire which destroyed most of the evidence. Edward Allard, a leading expert in FLIR (forward looking infrared recorder) stated his conclusions in a court document after reviewing the official FLIR footage of the final assault:

"11. At 12:08:32, the FLIR depicts events at the rear of the building, where the large 'gymnasium' structure has largely been demolished. Two very bright thermal flashes are visible near to or in the window at the center, in front of and to one side of the (armored vehicle) which is stopped there. I see no natural explanation for these flashes. They would not, for instance, be reflections of sunlight off glass...

I declare under penalty of perjury that the above is true and correct."

Source: www.indirect.com/www/dhardy/allard.html (Original source no longer available.)

Less than one minute after this hot, bright sustained flash occurred "in front of and to one side of the (armored vehicle)," the Mt. Carmel complex began the process of burning down. Fire department personnel on the scene were told they could not move forward to put out the fire until "the danger had passed." The FBI determined the danger had passed well after the building had burned to the ground.

* Who commanded "Operation Trojan Horse?"

Let's review the evidence that the US military was involved in the raid, siege, and final assault on the Branch Davidian complex outside of Waco, Texas:

1. The training, and probably the tactics, for the raid were designed by the Army and provided at its base in Ft. Hood, Texas.

2. At least some military vehicles were at or near the scene of the initial raid the day it occurred, and nine or more were stationed nearby no later than the day after.

3. Advanced "non-lethal" military tactics and technologies were used to surveil and harass the Branch Davidians in the complex and, as a result, the Mt. Carmel center quickly became a study destination for special forces officers from both the US and the UK.

4. The Justice Department admits at least 15 active duty personnel and 16 armored vehicles (and one tank retrieval vehicle) were involved in the operation.

5. Lethal quantities of toxic gas were used in the final assault, and FLIR video documentation shows that there was a bright flash in the front of one of the tanks used for spraying the gas less than one minute before the fire began.

6. Two unnamed high-ranking Army officers personally presented Attorney General Janet Reno with the final assault tactics for her, as chief law enforcement officer of the US, to sign off on.

It sure sounds like a military operation to me. If so, then who was the military commander behind Waco?

You can learn a lot from reading a man's resume, which may explain why the US news media has gone to such great pains to avoid even the suggestion that General Wesley K. Clark, Supreme Commander of NATO, had a life before his current exalted position. But he did, and here's his official bio from the NATO web site: www.shape.nato.int/Biographies/gen_CLARK/GEN_CLAR.htm (Original source no longer available.)

Clark was the Commander 1st Cavalry Division, Fort Hood, Texas from August 1992 to April 1994. The Mt. Carmel raid was on February 29, 1993. The arson-murders occurred April 19.

This means he would have been the officer who authorized and commanded the armored vehicles used in the raid, the siege, and the final assault. This alone is sufficient to make Clark a prime suspect, but there is much more.

Clark came to Fort Hood with an unusual background. He had been Commander of the National Training Center (October 1989-October 1991) and Deputy Chief of Staff for Concepts, Doctrine and Developments, US Army Training and Doctrine Command (TRADOC), Fort Monroe, Virginia (October 1991-August 1992) See: www.tradoc.army.mil

He was not your typical armor officer. If there were a high profile, cutting edge training exercise to be conducted at Ft. Hood, it probably would have been handled, if not initiated, by him.

Here's why:

TRADOC, where Clark was Deputy Chief right before becoming an armor commander at Ft. Hood, has as its primary mission to "prepare soldiers for war and design the army of the future." And what will that army look like?

Item number one from the TRADOC vision statement: "... enable America's Army to operate with joint, multinational and interagency partners across the full range of operations." This would include working with the ATF and FBI which would have put Clark in touch with the high-ranking officials in both agencies long before Waco.

Further, Clark's resume explains the mystery of the quick appearance of special forces study groups at Waco. His background - was there another officer at Ft. Hood with similar credentials? - gave him exactly the kind of clout and professional relationships needed to arrange for the hosting of special forces officers from the US and UK at the Mt. Carmel siege on such short notice.

* Clark's tactics re-emerge in Yugoslavia

There are many similarities between the war in Yugoslavia and "Operation Trojan Horse" at Waco, but most of them are part of the conduct of any US war. Here's a quick short list of seven:

1. Exert tight information control over a mostly cooperative US news media.

2. Attribute civilian casualty reports to "propaganda."

3. Declare that the attacks are for humanitarian purposes, to "stop the bad guy."

4. Break numerous agreements, then call the other side unreliable.

5. Offer absurd terms in negotiation sessions, hide these terms from the public, then punish the other side for its recalcitrance in failing to accept a "reasonable" settlement.

6. Coordinate a propaganda effort against the other side before the assault. (The Waco Tribune-Herald ran a two part smear piece against Koresh on Feb 27, 1993, the day before the raid, and on the morning of, entitled, "The Sinful Messiah.")

7. Accuse the other side of being responsible for crimes they did not commit.

In addition to these commonly used tactics, there are a few similarities in tactics between Waco and Yugoslavia that show Clark's unique stamp:

1. Symbolic destruction of property dear to the "bad guy"

Yugoslavia: Milosevic's private home was bombed repeatedly, in spite of the fact that it was not a military target and was located in a residential neighborhood.

Waco: Tank operators repeatedly rolled over and destroyed numerous vehicles belonging to the church which Karesh, an avid car mechanic, had personally worked on.

2. Obsession with silencing the victim's "propaganda"

Yugoslavia: Clark repeatedly bombed Yugoslavian television and radio transmitters and stations, even though NATO had promised in writing not to attack stations. Several workers were killed in these attacks. Clark declared them "legitimate military targets," though their only function was news reporting and entertainment.

Waco: One of the first acts of post-raid Waco was cutting off the complex's phone system to anyone but the FBI and disabling its short wave radio system. As the siege wore on, the electricity was also cut off, turned back on, then cut off again.

3. Mislabeling the nature of the attacking force

Yugoslavia: The war was painted as a NATO operation. In reality, the vast majority of funding, manpower, aircraft, targeting, and munitions were provided by the US and the operation was commanded by a US general. The entire operation was in violation of the NATO charter, US law, and the UN Charter.

Waco: The assault was painted as an ATF, then FBI operation. In reality, the training, tactics, equipment, and essential manpower were provided by the US military and the operation was commanded by a US general. The entire operation was in violation of US law.

4. Failure to plan for obvious contingencies

Yugoslavia: No meaningful preparations were made for the likelihood of large numbers of refugees, who, after all, the war was supposedly being fought on behalf of. However, immense military power was arranged for.

Waco: No ambulance was on call during the initial raid in spite of the fact that over 100 armed agents were involved and the complex housed numerous women and children as well as men who were thought to be armed. However, a convoy of armored vehicles was provided as a "backup."

5. Assuming the victims would "fold" immediately to a massive show of force

Yugoslavia: It took over 70 days of terror bombing and attacks on basic life support services to win a surrender. Clark initially predicted settlement in a matter of days.

Waco: Mt. Carmel residents, who, in keeping with rural Texas culture, were well armed (they were also legally licensed gun dealers), returned fire on the attacking ATF agents, killing four of them. They then held out for another 50 days until being gassed and burned alive.

(It's important to note that the ATF agents continued firing until they completely ran out of ammunition. They then had to retreat one mile across an open field. Not a single shot was fired by the Branch Davidians during their retreat.)

6. Non-combatants were killed in large numbers "by accident" using the most vicious of weapons - video evidence of assaults were "lost" due to unlikely technical problems

Yugoslavia: Clark's PR people claim the flight camera malfunctioned in the US warplane that killed 87 Albanian refugees in Korisa in Kosovo. Clark's extensive use of cluster bombs and his targeting of hospitals and other health care facilities, including old age homes and maternity wards, is well documented

Waco: Key video taken during the initial raid was declared "not shot" because, say ATF officials, the Branch Davidians "jammed" their video camera operations with "radio signals." (Video people know this is ridiculous.) The footage from other videos and still pictures, official and unofficial, taken during the raid also "disappeared." The gas attack on the residents of Mt. Carmel was sheer savagery.

7. And last but not least: tactical incompetence on an epic scale, driven by Clark's desire to have his accomplishments recorded for posterity on video

Yugoslavia: Clark stopped the movement of British troops into Kosovo to give unprepared US troops a chance to get in place for a triumphant televised liberation scene. Meanwhile, the Russian army, which Clark was trying to keep out of the

Kosovo "peacekeeping" mission, marched in and secured the province's key strategic area, the airport at Pristina.

Waco: Local television news media were informed of the Mt. Carmel raid the day before and by showing up at the scene (one news van got lost and reportedly asked neighbors where the raid was), removed the surprise element and completely undermined the raid.

The bottom line on Clark's modus operandi:

Murder innocent civilians with cold-blooded viciousness for personal and political gain, add heavy doses of military incompetence, then sell it to the President, who is apparently an eager buyer.

This is the man Bill Clinton - who like Clark is 50-something, an Arkansas native, and a Rhodes Scholar - would like to make commander-in-chief for the defense of the continental U.S.

In the meantime, he intends to be supreme commander of "peacekeeping" efforts in Kosovo.

One last thing about Clark.

In between Waco and Yugoslavia:

"General Clark's last assignment was as Commander-in-Chief, United States Southern Command, Panama, from June 1996 to July 1997, where he commanded all U.S. forces and was responsible for the direction of most U.S. military activities and interests in Latin America and the Caribbean." The part of the world where the US has raised military, police, and paramilitary (death squad) collaboration to a high art.

More on Waco:

www.waco93.com

Full text of this article appears at:

www.brasscheck.com/clarkatwaco.html

Bait and Switch: The reality of the NATO/KLA Alliance emerges after the Yugoslavian pullout

June 15, 1999

* NATO is deputizing armed KLA in some areas, looking the other way in others as they rampage

* The coal mines of Kosovo: KLA forces led by MPRI-associate Croatian General Agim Ceku seize key strategic coal reserves in Kosovo

The KLA was supposed to put down its arms as part of the peace agreement which started the withdrawal of Yugoslavian forces from the Yugoslavian province of Kosovo.

Before the NATO bombing, the KLA, a "terrorist organization" according to the US State Department (1998) and funded by criminal enterprises, including the heroin trade and extortion according to Interpol, had been waging a guerilla terror campaign in Kosovo targeting primarily civilians, including uncooperative Albanians.

By all reports, Yugoslavian forces are withdrawing according to schedule, but guess who's moving into the vacuum created by their departure? Armed KLA forces - with the endorsement of NATO.

Here's today's line from the AP, which less than a week ago was repeating NATO assurances that the KLA would disarm: "Ethnic Albanian rebels are quietly moving in, taking positions vacated by departing Serbs as the West struggles to reach an agreement with Russia on the operation of the massive peacekeeping mission."

The use of language here is remarkable. The armed terrorist KLA moves "quietly" and the diplomatic dispute between Russian and NATO is a "struggle." Add to this the fact that these two issues are in no way logically connected and you have a first class piece of propaganda.

Source: Yahoo! News

It looks like the presence of 200 Russian troops at an airport General Wesley Clark says he had no plans for is about to be used by NATO as the justification for open collaboration with the KLA in some parts of Kosovo.

"Good" KLA members have been given yellow armbands by NATO to show that they are authorized "peacekeepers." In some areas where the KLA is openly resuming its terror campaign, NATO commanders in the field are doing nothing and the Supreme Commander and his PR flacks just shrug and call the situation "difficult":

"Brigadier General Fritz von Korff said that Nato has no mandate for disarming the KLA, and that it would require a separate resolution from the UN. `For the moment, I can only disarm a KLA soldier if he hinders me in fulfilling my mission,' he said. At the moment, KLA is controlling Pec, Prizren and Orahovac, although its demilitarization was required by the agreement."

Source: INET (INET is a group of Yugoslavian computer engineers who have been issuing near hourly bulletins on news of the war. They were the first to report the movement of Russian troops out of Bosnia and have generally been days to weeks ahead of the US news media reports, and far more reliable.)

Also reported by INET today:

1. An explosion at Pristina airport where the Russians are stationed. In a report yesterday, the AP relayed a thinly veiled threat from the KLA that it "could not guarantee the safety of the Russian troops." A Russian military spokesman attributed the explosion to a mortar round.

2. Reports from the Russian press indicate that Bulgaria has approved use of its airspace by Russian planes. The Russian RIA news agency reports that the arrival of 7,000 Russian paratroopers from Pskov is expected in Kosovo in the next few days. (I'm double checking this number. It's awfully high. If it's correct, they're not coming to play games.)

3. At a press conference yesterday, Sali Mustafer, KLA commander for Pristina, stated that the ultimate aim of the KLA was to unite all the Albanian people in one homeland, including areas of Macedonia. More on this later.

And the following essential points go selectively unmentioned in most US news reports:

1. Thousands of Serbian civilians are fleeing their homes in Kosovo in fear of a KLA attack.

2. KLA assaults and provocations, including several shooting deaths, which target civilians as well as Yugoslavian military and police are being reported from all over the province.

***

The Coal Mines of Kosovo

Coal may not seem like an important resource in the age of oil and silicon, but for poorer countries that are lucky enough to have some, it's essential for industry and maintaining basic life support systems. It gets cold in Belgrade in the winter. Cold enough for vulnerable people to freeze to death.

The LA Times reported yesterday that KLA forces took control of one of Kosovo's most important assets, the Belacevic coal mine.

"Serbian infantrymen who had guarded the Belacevic open pit mine during 16 months of guerrilla war pulled out at 8 a.m. Saturday. Their army's withdrawal from Kosovo was supposed to be tightly synchronized with the arrival of NATO-led troops to pacify the province. Instead, the advancing foot soldiers the mine director saw in his binoculars were from the Kosovo Liberation Army."

(I wonder who gave the KLA the timetable?)

Kosovo contains the largest coal reserves in the entire Balkans. NATO has already announced via a recent New York Times article that Kosovo will be economically cut off from Yugoslavia. The Kosovo coal reserves, so important to the economy of Yugoslavia, have in essence, been appropriated.

NATO appears to be completely unconcerned by the seizure of this asset valued in the hundreds of millions of dollars:

"Although the mine takeover was reported on Serbian radio and television Saturday, the peacekeepers knew nothing about it....

'I'm going to send a report to the guys in headquarters, and they'll probably have some questions,' (the Canadian area commander) told the mine director. 'Then they'll make a decision.'

An hour later, the lieutenant was still waiting for instructions. He explained that the British army unit he had contacted said it did not have jurisdiction of the area around the mine. He was trying to call someone else."

Source: Los Angeles Times, June 14, 1999

Unlike the typical sloppy hit and run terror tactics the KLA is known for, this operation was carried out with military precision.

Lost in the shuffle of the Kosovo story is the name and background of the KLA's military commander-in-chief. Here's a man you'd think would receive a fair amount of media attention. Yet he's almost as well kept a secret as the details of Wesley Clark's tour of duty at Ft. Hood, Texas during the Waco atrocity.

From the Brasscheck report of May 15:

"Jane's Defense Weekly... in the May 10 issue reports that the current leader of the Kosovo Liberation Army is a Croatian general, Agim Ceku. He was in charge of Operation 'Storm,' the bloodiest and most brutal military campaign - until the current NATO bombing - carried out in the Balkans since the invasion of the Nazis during World War II. In August 1995, the Operation 'Storm' offensive against the Serbian population in the Krajina region in Croatia drove hundreds of thousands of Serbs from the region that they have inhabited for centuries.

Ceku is a U.S.-trained military officer who is closely tied to the Pentagon's Military Professional Resources, Inc. (MPRI). The MPRI is a semi-official Pentagon contractor, headed by retired U.S. military officers. It specializes in sending mercenary armies under Pentagon contracts into unofficial wars. The MPRI was contracted by the Pentagon to organize and train the Croatian Army for its Operation Storm against Serbs in Krajina. This massive ground offensive against hundreds of thousands of civilians was seen as the decisive military event that forced the Milosevic government in Yugoslavia to sign the U.S.- brokered Dayton Accord for Bosnia."

Source: "Is the U.S./NATO leadership planning a ground war?" Brian Becker, Co-Director, International Action Center

One of MPRI's competitors in the brave new world of privatized and unaccountable military forces is a South African company called Executive Outcomes. The company, which operates primarily in Africa, has been known to take its fee in the shares of mines it has helped capture.

Finally, if you're wondering what a greater Albania would look like, here's an excerpt of an intelligence report from Jane's on the state of that country and the nature of the people who run it:

"After the collapse of the pyramid finance scheme in 1997, economic activity in Albania had been dominated by a few families who ran the country's organized crime gangs. Their reaction to the current crisis was strategic in nature. Orders went out that NATO troops were not to be attacked and middlemen were dispatched to set up deals to supply the incoming armies and aid agencies with food and other resources as well as rented buildings and land. Hundreds of millions of dollars are now pouring into the country.

In late April the Albanian telephone authorities switched off the international roaming facilities of the mobile phone network, forcing foreigners to buy special chips for more than US$1,000 to give their cell phones access to the world network.

Aid shipments into Tirana airport are also 'fair game,' and these generate huge 'kick-backs' for officials working there. Reputedly the job of chief police officer at the airport can be bought from a government official for a bribe of US$250,000, but the incumbent is only allowed to stay in the post for three months until the job is sold to someone else. As one NATO officer in Tirana commented: 'The Albanians now only have one god: money.'"

And this from Sam Smith, (www.prorev.com):

"BALKAN BELIEVE IT OR NOT

- Yugoslavia is actually a sovereign country.

- Kosovo is actually a province of Yugoslavia.

- Historically, the term for what is now happening in Kosovo is not 'peacekeeping mission' but 'invasion and occupation.'

- One way to tell this is to ask a simple question: just who asked NATO to bomb and invade Yugoslavia?"

For war criminals: There's no place like home

June 17, 1999

* For war criminals: there's no place like home

* Now they tell us

* Trying to sort out the latest Kosovo news

* Spanish pilots say NATO ordered civilian attacks

Where war criminals get their training

Seamus Martin, editor of the Irish Times, responded to Brass Check's piece on NATO's Gen. Clark with this comment:

"(Clark's) subordinate Gen Sir Michael Jackson was an officer in the British Parachute regiment during the Bloody Sunday massacre in Northern Ireland."

It seems that being involved in civilian atrocities at home is an effective way to ensure advancement in the US and UK armed forces.

There is a historical precedent for this. In 1935, General Douglas MacArthur authored a field manual offering directions for handling labor demonstrations and other social unrest. It was called "Military Aid in Civil Disturbances." According to George Seldes, it became a guidebook not only for the US Army but also for the National Guard and various vigilante groups that were involved in "suppressing strikes and disturbances during the Great Depression."

MacArthur's advice for handling strikers:

- "...all efforts should be made if the use of gas is contemplated to supply plenty of it."

- "...airplanes may be used for the purpose of keeping rioters off roofs by means of machine-gun fire."

- "...armored cars will be especially valuable in riot duty."

And this gem, which Seldes characterizes as the "Shoot to Kill" order:

"Blank cartridges should never be used against a mob."

MacArthur developed the material for his manual during various domestic operations, including the gassing of fellow WWI veterans during the Bonus Army encampment in Washington DC in 1932.

Now they tell us

Buried way back (A35) in today's Washington Post:

"The KLA had a simple, but effective, plan. It would kill Serb policemen. The Serbs would retaliate, Balkan style, with widespread reprisals and the occasional massacre. The West would get more and more appalled, until finally it would -- as it did in Bosnia -- take action. In effect, the United States and much of Europe would go to war on the side of the KLA."

How many lives would have been saved if this had been on the front pages 80 days ago? I wonder why the Washington

Post took so long to, quite timidly, publish this honest and common sense report on the roots of the Kosovo crisis.

Too busy flacking for the Pentagon, I guess.

Of course, it's not quite as simple as the Post presents it. Not mentioned as part of the KLA's "simple plan": 1) major PR support from the AP and other US news outlets and 2) coordination with NATO command before, during, and after the bombing. The current head of the KLA forces is a Pentagon trained Croatian general, Agim Ceku, who earned his spurs killing Serb civilians in "Operation Storm" in August of 1995.

Also today, while US news outlets higlighted a single dramatic episode of NATO troops disarming KLA terrorists - in a non-strategic area - Reuters sent out this, mostly ignored, photo showing armed KLA members marching into a Kosovo town with US armor providing escort.

Trying to sort out the Kosovo news

Silvia from www.keepfaith.com writes:

"... there are at least four versions of every story, when searched globally - from Australian, to British, to the US press and so on.

Sample - The two Serbs killed by the NATO troops in the small yellow car were: two Serbian suicide bombers, two drunken soldiers shooting in the air, KLA.

Kacanic mass graves were: discovered by British paratroopers, shown to NATO by KLA, shown to NATO by a girl carrying flowers.

They were: 28 bodies in a covered up well that a KLA fighter refused to show to the present journalist, 81 individual graves, numbered but not named that the Yugo soldiers took out of a mass grave, autopsied and reburied individually before retreating, about 90 individual graves that the British soldiers saw the local Albanians rebury, all men from 18-35 years, men, women and children, including three nurses, including two nurses - and this is just from the Western press."

Spanish War Pilots Claim NATO Ordered Attacks on Civilian Targets

(Note: I don't know anything about "Articulo 20." I do know that the Spanish military have been resentful of their treatment by NATO and there have been several interesting leaks to Spanish newspapers of internal NATO documents relating to the Yugoslavian assault. One, a PR strategy document, called for the use of "focus groups" with "friendly journalists" to help NATO devise ways to "tell its story better.")

The following article indicates there may be some pilots willing to come forward and speak on the subject of NATO's targeting procedures. It will be interesting to see what, if anything, comes of this.

ARTICULO 20 (SPAIN-WEEKLY)

By Jose Luis Morales (?) - June 14, 1999

The pilots of Spanish planes who participated in bombing raids against Yugoslavia do not feel like "supermen" nor masters of aerospace. Quite the contrary, they say that our forces play to the tune of music played by the North Americans, and accuse NATO of having honoured with medals the bombing of civilian targets, what they otherwise name "collateral damages."

Captain Adolfo Luis Martin de la Hoz, who returned to Spain at the end of May after having participated in the bombings from the beginning, an "authentic expert for the dreadful F-18," the war plane most often used in the war strategy of "scorched land" in the Balkans, is very categoric: "First of all, I want to make it clear that the majority, I say the majority, of my colleagues, even if not all, are against the war in general and against this war of barbarity in particular."

Martin de la Hoz says that he and his colleagues "are burnt out."

"A few days ago, there appeared in the papers certain statements of Commander Maches Michavilla, who is now in the air base at Aviano with the pilots who replaced us, in which he said that our main helper in the air was mental and physical health. But I tell you that our worst enemies are our own authorities, the Defence Minister and all his team, the members of the Government, who know nothing about war and go along with it without informing themselves about anything and, what is gravest, who are guilty of lying to the Spanish people through the papers, radio and television, foreign correspondents and press agencies."

The suspicions that NATO's repeated bombings of civilian victims and non-military targets are not the result of war "errors," are confirmed by Captain Martin de la Hoz:

"Several times our colonel protested to NATO chiefs as to why they select targets which are not military targets. They threw him out with curses, saying that we should know that the North Americans would lodge a complaint to the Spanish Army, once through Brussels and again to the Defence Minister. But there is more, and I want to tell it to the whole world: once there was a coded order from the North American military that we should drop anti-personnel bombs over the localities of Prishtine (Pristina) and Nish (Nis). The colonel refused it altogether and, a couple of days later, the transfer order came. But what I say now is nothing compared to what I shall have to say when the time comes."

The Spanish military denounces that "the Spanish Government not only does not try to inform themselves, but that they also accept the false reports that are edited for them in Aviano, where there is a sort of military press cabinet in the hands of North American generals and functionaries. Ever since we arrived in Italy" - the captain goes on - "there is no end to humiliations and insults. The only order-givers are the North American generals, and no one else. We are zeroes, just as our replacements are going to be."

"But there is still more to that. Here, they say that several operations were directed by Spanish commanders and pilots. Lies over lies. All the missions that we flew, every single one, were planned by high U.S. military authorities. Even more, they were all planned in detail, including attacking planes, targets and type of ammunition that we have to drop. We never directed anything, and our missions were limited to flying over the borders of Macedonia, Albania, Bosnia and Slovakia (Slovenia?)."

Government's lies

None of the pilots presently stationed at Aviano, who replaced those who went to the Italian base shortly before the start of war, last March 23, were there with a clear conscience, says the Spanish military.

"It is being written to saturation that the disciplined and patriotic Spanish pilots" - according to Minister Eduardo Serra - "are concentrating on the complexity of their war missions".

"But we read so many discrepancies, so many lies, that we agreed to not read a single newspaper until we return. Our anger is enormous. The President of the government, the Minister of Foreign Affairs and the Defence Minister are lying brazenly each time they talk about the war. Some of us are of another opinion and believe that they do not inform themselves, because the North Americans - the White House, the Pentagon, the CIA, the Embassy or military information service, whoever, do not inform them about anything. How should they inform themselves if our own Javier Solana has not informed himself since the war broke out?

Solana is a puppet who has been put there by the Yanquis to do what they tell him he must do. And so he does, standing straight before General Clark when he talks to him, or better said, when he issues him the orders that he has to implement without delay."

On the subject of manipulation of war information, Captain de la Hoz says that "no one has said anything about the incidents that took place in Aviano, about the disastrous maintenance of Spanish machines, about everything, and about the constant humiliations to which we were subjected from the beginning.

Not that we are cannon fodder. No. We are nothing. About the fatal accidents, the losses suffered without connection to combat, the contempt and the sanctions, not a word. From no one!"

For the wrong selection of targets and humiliations, the Spanish military are ever more certain that there is no alibi.

"We know perfectly well that we are intervening in a conflict" - says Martin de la Hoz - "which is rejected by the majority of the Spanish people and this is most important for us. But what they do not say in any information, commentary or speech, is that the Spanish, Dutch, Portuguese... that we are there to cover for the North American generals who are wheeling and dealing in the war.

There is no journalist who has the slightest idea what is happening in Yugoslavia. They are destroying the country, bombing it with new weapons, toxic nerve gases, surface mines dropped by parachute, bombs containing uranium, napalm, sterilization chemicals, sprayings to poison the crops and weapons of which even we still do not know anything.

The North Americans are committing there, one of the biggest barbarities that can be committed against humanity. Many very bad things will be told in the future about what was happening there because, by the way, judging by what we talked about with the British and German officers, it was designed in order to divide the Europeans and keep us subjected for many decades."

Therefore, Captain Martin de la Hoz is enraged when there is talk about the costs of the war. There should be no doubts, he confirms, that the military detached in Aviano are receiving bonuses which "multiply by five our salary, but not considering the daily expenses and other perquisites. We could say that we should be satisfied with what this war means economically for each one of us, but it is not true, what they give us is chocolate for the parrots.

This war is going to cost the Spaniards more than all the money allocated for culture in the last five years. And, even if now no one says anything because of the elections, it will come in a few months and will be felt in our pockets. Because this brutal Yanqui-only war, no one's but the Yanquis, is going to be paid by all of us.

Be certain that what I say is not to exculpate myself and to intone 'mea culpa' for having participated in it, because I will never be able to forget that what was being committed there was one the biggest savageries of history."

Experimental weapons used in Yugoslavia and elsewhere

June 18, 1999

1. A reader points out that Douglas MacArthur was not the only war hero shooting at and gassing fellow veterans during the 1932 demonstrations in Washington D.C. Dwight D. Eisenhower was also involved in the operation. He's the president who warned us on his last day in office to watch out for the "military industrial complex."

Since the winners get the privilege of writing history, few people are aware of the bombing attacks on German civilian targets that were a regular feature of World War II. In the city of Dresden for example, a non-military target, tens of thousands of civilians were killed in just one night as the result of an Allied bombing raid testing an experimental technique designed to induce a firestorm large enough to engulf an entire city.

2. Yes, the US Army was involved at Waco - and the operation had formal approval of the Joint Chiefs of Staff.

An Army memo dated May 13, 1993 for the Commander U.S. Army Special Operations Command, Fort Bragg, NC summarized a meeting held April 14, 1993 between the FBI, the Justice Department, and Army officials. The names of the latter were blacked out.

Quote:

"The meeting began with an explanation by the (Army) scientist on the effects of CS... His assessment was that CS was non-lethal and presented very little physical threat to the Branch Davidian occupants..."

(Brasscheck note: "CS concentrations in the rooms directly injected by the M5 delivery (Army tank) alone ranged from 2 to 90 times that required to deter trained soldiers.

Methylene chloride concentrations in the rooms directly injected by gas were as high as 1.8 times the IDLH [Immediately Dangerous to Life and Health] concentration and nearly to the concentration that would render a person unconscious." - Failure Analysis Associates report on Waco)

More from the post-mortem US Army memo on Waco:

"Prior to deployment all DELETED were advised as to the legal restrictions on the nature and scope of assistance they could provide to the FBI and other law enforcement agencies. Their activities fell within these boundaries. All support to the HRT (hostage rescue team) was approved by the Joint Chiefs of Staff."

The current print edition of Counter Punch has an article devoted to this story. (www.counterpunch.com)

3. References to experimental weapons used in the assault on Yugoslavia are starting to pile up, though no one has yet issued a comprehensive report on the "nonconventional weapons" used there.

As a recent Le Monde article points out, use of these weapons is usually kept secret and denied until overwhelming forces compel admission.

For example, it wasn't until late April that a NATO spokesman confirmed that depleted uranium (DU) rounds were being used in Yugoslavia as they had been in the Gulf War. Here's what that means for the civilians returning to their homes - not to mention the NATO peacekeeping troops:

"It was only with the revelations about 'friendly fire' that the US was forced publicly to admit the use of DU armaments during the Gulf war. During Operations Desert Shield and Desert Storm, 29 American vehicles were contaminated by DU on the battlefield. Twenty-one of them (6 Abrams tanks and 15 Bradley combat vehicles) had been damaged by these munitions. In total 15 soldiers were killed and more than 60 injured by fire from DU arms. Since Iraq did not possess these kinds of weapons, it was obvious that the damage must have been a result of targeting errors by US troops. The Army Times (the US army's official newspaper) of 26 July 1993 published a detailed list of damage sustained as a result of 'friendly fire' without, however, saying anything about deaths that may have occurred after the event.

Five years after the war, 30 of the soldiers who had been victims of this 'collateral damage' were checked by the Depleted Uranium Program at the MD VA Medical Centre in Baltimore. Fifteen still presented with a high level of radioactivity in their urine. Dietz subsequently carried out a study into DU contamination effects among Gulf war veterans and noted that 'If you've got any indication of DU at this late date, even at low levels, it would indicate you'd had a pretty heavy dose five years ago!' But he adds that 'the US army and the Department of Veterans' Affairs have shown an unwillingness to investigate health issues associated with the toxicity and radioactivity of inhaled and ingested DU aerosol particles that have become absorbed in the body. Both have refused to test large numbers of veterans for the presence of DU in their bodies.'

Devastating effects

Nevertheless, it is by now accepted that some of the pathologies listed as 'Gulf war syndrome' were actually due to the presence of DU. The International Action Center, set up by the former US attorney general, Ramsey Clark, has been very active against the Gulf war, campaigning for the embargo against Iraq to be lifted. One of its members, Sara Flounders, reports that the Department of Veterans' Affairs has carried out a study among 251 veterans' families in Mississippi. Since the war, 67% of them have had children with serious abnormalities.

There has been an increase in certain cancers and hitherto unknown congenital malformations - and exactly the same has been reported, on an alarming scale, from Iraq. It is difficult to evaluate the exact quantity of DU armaments that were used in Iraq, Kuwait and Saudi Arabia. According to the US armed forces, more than 14,000 rounds were used by US troops, of which 7,000 were during training in the Saudi Arabian desert prior to the war and 3,000 were lost during a fire at a US Army arms dump at Doha in Kuwait. Ammunition used by the British, and probably other armed forces, needs to be added to the count.

A secret report from Britain's Atomic Energy Authority, made public in November 1991, indicates that at least 40 tons of DU were left in the desert by the Allied forces. It notes the presence in Kuwait and Iraq of enough uranium to cause '500,000 potential deaths.' Nine years after the end of the conflict, Iraqi doctors are still reporting abnormally high incidences of leukaemia among children, tumours and cancers among adults, and births or abortions of foetuses with monstrous abnormalities."

Source: Le Monde Diplomatique, June 1999

Kosovo is KLA country now

June 22, 1999

Following the well established pattern of: lie with a headline, retract with a back-of-the-paper story; NATO and the AP reported that a "Serb booby-trap" killed two UK peacekeepers and two "civilians" who were clearing a school complex. This led a senior UK military official to say it will be "at least five years" before all the Yugoslav mines and booby-traps are cleared from Kosovo.

One problem with the story: the device was not a "Serb booby-trap" but a US-made, NATO-dropped cluster bomb. The AP finally got around to accurately reporting this today.

And the "civilians?" They turned out to be KLA members - working alongside UK troops. And no one yet has commented on the fact that there were US-made cluster bombs littering a school yard. Too common to be considered news any more?

The KLA, on whose behalf it now appears NATO fought the war, is showing its stripes. Declared a terrorist organization by the US State Department in 1998, the group has long been known to be an equal opportunity criminal organization, killing Serbians, Gypsies, and fellow Albanians without discrimination.

I guess when the KLA kills fellow Albanians, it's not "ethnic cleansing" and therefore nothing for Clinton & Co. to be concerned with. No racial or ethnic hatred involved. Just pure murder. KLA "peacetime" atrocities are occurring with such frequency now that even the AP is compelled to report the more ghastly incidents (quietly). Here's one you may not have seen:

June 18, 1999

PRIZREN, Yugoslavia (AP) - German soldiers detained 25 ethnic Albanian rebels today after finding one elderly man dead and more than 15 others hurt in a police station that had been under control of the Kosovo Liberation Army since early this week.

Most of the victims seemed to be ethnic Albanians or Gypsies between the ages of 50 and 60, said Lt. Col. Dietmar Jeserich, a spokesman for the German army serving in the Kosovo peace force in the region.

During the Kosovo conflict that started February 1998 and ended in a peace deal last week, the KLA had assassinated not only Serbs, but also ethnic Albanians and Gypsies believed loyal to the Belgrade regime of Slobodan Milosevic.

(Editor's note: "Loyal to the regime?" Is that like the "regime" of Bill Clinton or Tony Blair? Appalling as he may be, Milosevic is an elected official of a sovereign country. Is it possible that the latest victims of KLA terror are merely law abiding citizens who refused to support criminals and criminal acts?)

One man in his 70s was found dead, chained to a chair. He appeared to have died shortly before the German soldiers arrived, Jeserich said.

Most of the injured had bloody wounds and bruises, many on their faces. One man had huge purple welts across his back. Two or three others had what appeared to be stab wounds in their legs...

German troops found a stash of weapons, including grenades, machine guns, mortars and shells. They also found heavy wooden sticks and spikes with nails that they said appeared to be “instruments of torture.”

The New York Times showed some of the victims with massive welts on their backs and faces, with a caption cautiously stating they "appear to have been beaten."

The 25 KLA detainees were permitted to go free after being held for a short time.

From a US military source: "NATO has no authority to detain KLA members."

So, let's get this straight. No police, a few thousand NATO troops muddling around trying to find their way, black uniformed terrorists in control of scores of villages and key economic infrastructure, torturing and murdering at will - and no one in the province has the authority to do anything other than disarm them.

None of this is enough to deter the New York Times and other US news media from giving the KLA front page legitimacy. After all, now that the province has been torn away by bombardment from the country of which it was legally part, who else is going to run the country?

And to make sure they do it right...

"Just one week after President Clinton explained that he authorized a military attack to enforce ethnic amity in the Balkans, the Senate Appropriations Committee last Thursday quietly and unanimously voted for $20 million in start-up money to equip a Kosovo 'self-defense force.' It definitely will not be in the business of promoting good feelings between Albanian and Serb.

The Clinton administration made no objection to the appropriation pressed by Sen. Mitch McConnell (R KY). While insisting it was not a continuation of his long crusade to arm the Kosovo Liberation Army, McConnell told me 'some of those folks' in the new U.S.-trained police force will be KLA guerrilla fighters."

Robert Novak - June 21, 1999

Just plain "folks"...

Note that when KLA members commit atrocities, it's "rogue elements" who are responsible, but when Yugoslavian forces are involved (and oddly, hard documentation of KLA atrocities is still, at this late date, much, much easier to come by), the orders must always have come directly from the top government officials in Belgrade. Does this make Bill Clinton responsible for the anti-war protestor in Santa Cruz, California who was recently assaulted with near deadly force by uniformed police officers of his "regime?"

More on KLA as a military power in Kosovo from a Reuters report (6/22/99):

"The Serb-dominated civil administration has completely collapsed, the police are gone, and nothing has been established to replace their functions, apart from the NATO peacekeeping force, which is being stretched in all directions...

In remote parts of Kosovo, its black-uniformed military police are now the only law, and its soldiers guard factories and other valuable installations. They are trusted by Kosovo Albanians and it would be counter-productive to remove them from the scene before NATO is able to take over the responsibilities."

Note: The last people to wear black uniforms in this part of the world were associates of Adolph Hitler.

And this war which killed so many civilians, and has created a terrorist-controlled state, policed by black uniformed thugs who are subject to no authority, how well did it succeed in damaging the Yugoslavian forces in Kosovo?

"Nato officers have been astonished that thousands of Yugoslav tanks, missile launchers, artillery batteries, personnel carriers and trucks have been withdrawn from the province with barely a scratch on them." - The Independent (UK) 6/21/99

Astonished? Why? Brasscheck readers knew NATO was hitting nothing but civilians nearly a month ago, and *why* - and NATO knew it too:

"Why such an abysmal performance by NATO? Because tanks, artillery, and ACV's are the easiest things in the world to hide. They can be put in caves, barns, warehouses, truck trailers, underground parking lots, covered with camouflage and stashed in the woods, or just put under tarps. Hiding equipment is basic military procedure. NATO knew this going into this 'war'

Destroyed or damaged (so far):

70 tanks (out of 1,025)

130 ACVs (out of 850)

130 artillery (out of 3,750)

80 planes (out of 155)"

Source: "The stats NATO doesn't want you to see" Brasscheck - May 26, 1999

All about the KLA: Special Report (by Sam Smith)

June 23, 1999

UNDERNEWS SPECIAL

Fun Facts About Our New Allies

Sam Smith

June 22, 1999

The Progressive Review

***

FUN FACTS ABOUT OUR NEW ALLIES

-- Hashim Thaqi, now mildly referred to in media like the Washington Post as the leader of the provisional Kosovo government, is a 29-year-old precocious KLA warlord known in the field as "Snake." Putting him in charge of the reconstruction of Kosovo is a bit like having let General Patton run the Marshall Plan or having a Contra leader coordinate post-hurricane aid to Central America.

-- Thaqi, a radical university student who helped to organize the KLA, rose to the top in early March by liquidating the more democratic and moderate government-in-exile of the moderate reconciliationist, Ibrahim Rugova. Rugova had been elected shadow president during a 1992 rump election but received little support from the US or NATO and was not recognized by Yugoslavia. While there is no evidence of direct American involvement in Thaqi's elevation, Madeleine Albright quickly hailed him with a State Department announcement declaring KLA's support of the Rambouillet surrender terms "a welcome development and an important step forward in the negotiating process, one that furthers prospects for a peaceful resolution to the Kosovo conflict."

-- Thaqi had been a regional commander in the rebel army and was convicted in absentia by Yugoslav courts and sentenced to 22 years in prison. He has vowed to fight for Kosovo's independence although he is quite close to Albania. According to one regional news report this spring, Albania spokesman Sokol Quoka said that "Tirana had established contacts with the [KLA] long ago and that the organization was steering its activities to the political sphere. Quoka went on to say that Tirana had already given its support to Hasim Thaqi, the head of the Kosovo negotiating team in Paris, Adem Demaqi, Blerim Shala and Yakup Krasniqi."

-- GARY WILSON, INTERNATIONAL ACTION CENTER: The origins of the KLA are murky at best. Some say it was founded in 1993. Others put the organization's beginnings in 1996, when a letter was sent to the media announcing its formation. The letter took credit for a February 1996 massacre of Serbian refugees from the Krajina region of Croatia who had fled to Kosovo for safety. Throughout 1996 and 1997, most of the KLA attacks were on Albanians who it called "collaborators." These were Albanian opponents of the separatist movement in Kosovo.

The KLA was never an organization like the liberation armies well known around the world. It never had a recognized leadership. It never even had a spokesperson until last year. It never issued any documents or statements of purpose. It doesn't even have a newspaper or magazine.

The grouping that called itself the KLA at first was actually an odd assortment of various opponents of the Yugoslav government who joined together with gangsters, mercenaries and other opportunists. Those who called themselves KLA ranged from people claiming to be followers of Albania's former Marxist leader, Enver Hoxha, to those who claimed roots in the fascist, nationalist Greater Albanian organizations of the 1940s. It was a combination of convenience, with no central agreement on anything but their hatred of the Yugoslav government.

... In late 1997 and early 1998, there was a sudden shift. The KLA went through a "rapid and startling growth," according to a report in the April 25, 1998, New York Times. Foreign mercenaries, money and arms started to pour into the KLA. The erstwhile KLA bands were quickly overwhelmed by an influx of mercenaries coming from Germany and the United States, who quickly took over command. It took a year before a representative from Kosovo could be produced to represent the KLA publicly. The new KLA began serious military operations, not only killing isolated Albanian and Serbian individuals but attacking government buildings and police stations. This open warfare could only be stopped by strong police measures. But when the government forces responded, the U.S. and NATO powers accused them of repression. This became the excuse for their war on Yugoslavia.

-- CHRIS HEDGES, FOREIGN AFFAIRS: [The KLA inside Kosovo is] "led by the sons and grandsons of rightist Albanian fighters [from the] Skanderbeg volunteer SS division raised by the Nazis, or the descendants of the rightist Albanian kacak rebels who rose up against the Serbs 80 years ago. Although never much of a fighting force, the Skanderbeg division took part in the shameful roundup and deportation of the province's few hundred Jews during the Holocaust. The division's remnants fought Tito's Partisans at the end of the war, leaving thousands of ethnic Albanians dead. The decision by KLA commanders to dress their police in black fatigues and order their fighters to salute with a clenched fist to the forehead has led many to worry about these fascist antecedents."

-- FRANK VIVIANO, MOTHER JONES: The Kosovo Albanians -- are part of an immense tidal wave of desperation that will fuel organized crime recruiting long into the next century. Put simply, the world's stateless nations -- Kosovan Albanians, Kurds from Turkey and Iraq, Tamils from Sri Lanka, Chechens from Russia, Ibos and Ogoni from Nigeria, and hundreds of other tribes and ethnic groups whose names are not yet in the headlines -- are the army-in-waiting of the new criminal super state. Or the army already in the field, altering its composition at a rate that befuddles law enforcement authorities.

-- SENATOR MITCH MCCONNELL: I don't think we have to do a background check [on the KLA] any more than we did on the Contras.

-- Raymond Bonner of New York Times has written that Albania has become a major hub for the movement of heroin and cocaine into Western Europe. As for the KLA's politics, one European diplomat told Bonner, "We really don't know what they are. There is an Islamic component, a left-wing component and there are those who are just guerillas." Said another diplomat, "They are not a people we would feel comfortable getting too close to. It is not like they are the military wing of a democratic resistance movement."

-- While the CIA's role in the Balkan disaster is not clear, it appears certain that NATO's chief military ally in the war against Yugoslavia, the KLA, is deeply involved in the heroin trade. And as late as last year, the KLA was still listed by the State Department as a terrorist organization.

-- Jerry Seper has reported in the Washington Times that some members of the KLA, which has financed its war effort through the sale of heroin, were trained in terrorist camps run by international fugitive Osama bin Laden -- who is wanted in the 1998 bombing of two US embassies in Africa that killed 224 persons, including 12 Americans. Seper wrote:

"Recently obtained intelligence documents show that drug agents in five countries, including the United States, believe the KLA has aligned itself with an extensive organized crime network centered in Albania that smuggles heroin and some cocaine to buyers throughout Western Europe and, to a lesser extent, the United States...

"The Greek representative of Interpol reported in 1998 that Kosovo's ethnic Albanians were 'the primary sources of supply for cocaine and heroin in that country.' ... France's Geopolitical Observatory of Drugs said that the KLA was a key player in the rapidly expanding drugs-for-arms business and helped transport $2 billion worth of drugs annually into Western Europe. German drug agents have estimated that $1.5 billion in drug profits is laundered annually by Kosovo smugglers, through as many as 200 private banks or currency-exchange offices."

-- In July 1998, PBS Newshour reported that U.S. Vietnam War veterans were training KLA mercenaries in Albania.

-- Jane's Defense Weekly reported April 20: "Special forces involvement confirmed." The report also said that special units from Britain, the United States, France "and other NATO groups" were working undercover in Kosovo.

-- The April 18 London Sunday Telegraph reported that SAS, a unit of the British special forces, was running two KLA training camps near Tirana, the Albanian capital. The same report said that the KLA also has contact with the Virginia-based MPRI, a corporate supplier of mercenaries set up by top US military officers. MPRI also trained the Croatian Army that carried out a vicious campaign against Serbs in 1995. For more on this see the July 28, 1997, Nation magazine.

-- On April 8 the Party of Democratic Socialism in Germany, an opponent of the war, issued a report describing an alleged CIA covert operation named "Operation Roots" aimed at sowing ethnic divisions in Yugoslavia to encourage its breakup. The report claimed that this operation has been going on "since the beginning of Clinton's presidency." It was supposedly a joint operation with the German secret service, which also sought to destabilize Yugoslavia. The final objective "is the separation of Kosovo, with the aim of it becoming part of Albania; the separation of Montenegro, as the last means of access to the Mediterranean; and the separation of the Vojvodina, which produces most of the food for Yugoslavia. This would lead to the total collapse of Yugoslavia as a viable independent state." The report also asserts that the KLA was founded by the CIA with funding that was funneled through drug-smuggling operations in Europe.

-- GARY WILSON, INTERNATIONAL ACTION CENTER: The top commander of the so-called Kosovo Liberation Army is Agim Ceku, a brigadier general who took a leave from the Croatian Army in February ... In August 1995 Ceku presided over "Operation Storm," the massive bombing and displacement of hundreds of thousands of Serb farmers from the part of Croatia known as the Krajina ... Ceku's military career began in the Yugoslav Army. But after Croatia became a separate state under the reactionary leadership of Franjo Tudjman, he defected to the Croatian Army. Ceku, an ethnic Albanian, was then trained by the United States. He is closely tied to Military Professional Resources, Inc ... Jane's Defense Weekly describes Ceku as "one of the key planners of the successful 'Operation Storm.'" Many reports have shown in detail that MPRI planned and directed this operation in Krajina. "Operation Storm" was, until the current U.S. bombing, the bloodiest and most brutal military campaign in the Balkans since the Nazi invasion during World War II ... This March 21, the New York Times carried a front-page story about a report from the International War Crimes Tribunal in The Hague that characterized this attack as probably the most brutal event in the Balkans in the last decade. But no commentators picked up on this. The report was quickly forgotten.

THE PROGRESSIVE REVIEW

ssmith@igc.org

Editor: Sam Smith

The war's results

June 25, 1999

The problem: A terrorist insurgency funded by drug money created a heavy handed response from Yugoslavia's central government.

The US solution: Kill up to 2,000 civilians and injure thousands more, create $30 billion+ in infrastructure damage, work with and support the terrorists while driving all civil authorities out of the province. Then insert a few thousand foreign troops as "peacekeepers" and let the terrorists run wild. Deduct the costs from the US Social Security fund. Violate the War Powers Act. Declare a humanitarian victory.

***

What follows are a few of the results of the US led assault on Yugoslavia this spring. The New York Times and the AP are now beginning to report the obvious, after acting as cheerleaders for the war.

My comments noted with *

KLA CHIEFS KILLING OFF THEIR RIVALS

By Chris Hedges

New York Times News Service

June 25, 1999

The senior commanders of the Kosovo Liberation Army, which has signed an agreement with NATO to disarm, carried out assassinations, arrests and purges within their ranks to thwart potential rivals, say current and former commanders in the rebel army and some Western diplomats.

The campaign, in which as many as a half-dozen top rebel commanders were shot dead, was directed by Hashim Thaci* and two of his lieutenants, Azem Syla and Xhavit Haliti, these officials said. Thaci denied through a spokesman that he was responsible for any killings.

* You mean that nice boy who appeared in the Times a few days ago as a budding statesman? I'm sure the shooting deaths of six of his rivals in the past few days was a coincidence.

Although the United States has long been wary of the KLA, the rebel group has become the main ethnic Albanian power in Kosovo.

* Long been wary? Even the Times can't believe this. And how did the KLA become the main power in Kosovo? Could it be that bombing the civil authorities and driving them out of the province had something to do with it?

Rebel commanders supplied NATO with target information during the bombing campaign.* Now, after the war, the United States and other NATO powers have effectively made partners of Thaci and the KLA in the rebuilding of Kosovo. The agreement NATO signed with Thaci, for example, envisions turning the KLA into a civilian police force and leaves open the possibility that the KLA could become a provisional army modeled on the National Guard in the United States.**

* I guess the US wasn't so wary after all.

** Sounds so wholesome, doesn't it? Too bad Norman Rockwell isn't alive to paint black uniformed KLA police walking down Main Street in Pristina.

***

THE WORLD WILL HAVE TO FEED KOSOVO

By Donna Bryson

Associated Press Writer

Thursday, June 24, 1999; 5:06 p.m. EDT

CERNUSA, Yugoslavia (AP)

"The world will have to feed Kosovo this summer and on into the winter, because the devastation and disruption of war has made it impossible for its people to help themselves...

The flights of people into the hills, firefights across farmland and other disruptions* meant plantings were missed or delayed. Babbitt's United States Agency for International Development estimated in early June that there would be next to no Kosovo wheat crop this year. The region harvests an average of 300,000 tons of wheat in a normal year."

* Does random NATO bombing of everything but military targets count as a disruption? Amazing the contortions the AP goes through to avoid stating the obvious. I doubt even Pravda under Stalin was any more dishonest in the service of power.

World Food Program spokeswoman Christiane Berthiaume said Thursday that aerial surveys over the last week revealed that only 30 percent of Kosovo's arable land had been planted. It was too late in the year to plant any more, and at any rate the threat of land mines* was keeping farmers out of their fields, she said.

* And NATO cluster bombs which are by far the more serious problem.

In Kosovo, 60 percent of the population depends on agriculture for its living.*

* Another food self-sufficient region of the world destroyed by American ingenuity. Add US agribusiness to the long list of beneficiaries of the war.

A few points about this AP article:

1) Apparently the "world food experts" never heard of a thing called winter wheat which will be ready to harvest this summer because it was planted in the fall - before NATO went on its humanitarian rampage. 2) It is *not* too late to plant "any more" though it is pretty late for spring wheat and other grain crops. 3) If 30% of the arable land was planted, how does that translate into "next to no Kosovo wheat crop?" 4) It is not only the Kosovars who will face a food shortfall, so will Yugoslavia and all the other countries which depend on the region's surplus. 5) Sloppy reporting aside, the problem is serious and it started, and could have been predicted, the day the first bomb fell. Reporting it now as if it was just "discovered" by aerial photos has to be some kind of sick joke.

The LA Times, one of the few US papers that made an honest effort to report the facts of the conflict, ran a story today with this headline which says it all:

Ethnic Cleansing: Part Two

(Original source no longer available.)

It's about the widespread murders of Serbians, Gypsies, other ethnic minorities, as well as "uncooperative Albanians" in Kosovo by KLA members. The KLA always said it wanted an ethnically pure state in Kosovo, and it looks like, thanks to the Clinton Administration, they're going to get one, not to mention a secure base from which to administer their heroin trading enterprise, Europe's largest.

And the citizens of the United States paid for it, while their newspapers and TV news programs carefully tutored them as to why this immoral, illegal, irrational slaughter of innocents was all for a good cause.

***

"Crime is contagious. If the government becomes a lawbreaker, it breeds contempt of law; it invites every man to become a law unto himself; it invites anarchy. To declare that in the administration of the criminal law, the end justifies the means - to declare that the government may commit crimes in order to secure the conviction of a private citizen - would bring terrible retribution."

- Supreme Court Justice Brandeis, 1928

July, 1999

A soldier's tale

July 11, 1999

Missing from the news: the makeup and conduct of the Yugoslav military conscripts sent to Kosovo. This appears to be another case where the facts turned out to be the *exact opposite* of what was reported by the US news.

From a report by Uli Schmetzer that appeared in the Chicago Tribune, one of the few US papers that made an honest attempt to investigate actual conditions in Kosovo.

The news you probably didn't see:

1. Regular Yugoslavian army units not only were not involved in atrocities, but also protected Albanian villages against the same.

2. A disproportionate number of draftees called up for service in Kosovo were from regions that were anti-Milosevic, pro-peace, and living in harmony with their ethnic Albanian neighbors.

3. NATO probably knew the nature of the Kosovo force but made them the focus of its attack anyway.

4. Yugoslav forces in Kosovo, mostly made up of amateurs, easily deflected attacks on it by the US's multi-billion dollar air assault machine.

***

1. "Many Albanian refugees concede the Yugoslav army was not involved in atrocities, except for some rogue units. Some refugees said they felt safer when the army occupied their villages or towns. Often the killing, looting and burning had been carried out before the army arrived, or when army units moved out and armed Serb fanatics moved in."

* Another "unintended" consequence of NATO bombing, driving legitimate forces out of the region so the thugs could take over.

2. "The corporal says he was among the first to be drafted into the reserves, the mainstay of the Yugoslav army. He is a leading figure in the Civic Alliance of Serbia movement, a pacifist group opposed to the nationalist politics of Milosevic. Like most government critics, he was quickly drafted to the front in Kosovo.

"I guess the government hoped we'd all be killed. They even suggested on television we should be sent to the front with a gun trained on our backs, indicating we were all potential traitors. But all of us did our duty because we told ourselves we were not fighting for Milosevic but to save Serbia and Serb lives," he said.

Kraljevo, 60 miles from the border with Kosovo, is a small city and an anti-Milosevic stronghold with a population of 120,000, including surrounding villages. Yet 23,000* of its men were drafted to the front in the reserves and 41 of them were killed in Kosovo, perhaps the highest ratio of casualties of any town in Serbia."

* More than half the reported Yugoslav forces in Kosovo.

"In a town closely associated with ethnic Albanians for generations, the Kosovo crisis generated strong anti-war sentiment. Milicevic said he participated in 40 anti-war conferences and saw the war as a 'political game' before he was mobilized."

3. "Serbian troops, he said, scoffed at leaflets NATO dropped, urging Yugoslav forces to go home and supplying a list of war criminals in Kosovo.

"We were furious," he said. "In those early days the list did not mention Milosevic nor any high-ranking generals, but colonels and majors who we knew, just like our own commander, had nothing to do with the ethnic cleansing. How could you trust NATO after reading that list?"

* NATO's intelligence was so accurate it could identify low ranking officers and drop leaflets on the exact locations where their troops were stationed, but it didn't know that over half the force was drawn from anti-Milosevic, pro-peace regions? This defies belief. This report makes the KLA-NATO coordinated slaughter of several hundred Yugoslav troops *after* the surrender even more appalling.

4. "Milicevic recalled with undisguised glee how his unit cheered from its bunkers as NATO planes bombed fake Yugoslav tanks fitted with heat-generating devices to hoodwink heat-seeking missiles. Sometimes, he said, bombs fell on fake bridges spanning fake rivers made of black plastic sheeting.

After the attacks, he said, the soldiers propped up the decoys, reactivated them, and watched as warplanes came back to blast them again with laser-guided electronic eye bombs. There was a celebration in the trenches, he said, when his unit shot down an unmanned NATO reconnaissance plane with a World War II anti-aircraft gun.

'We felt good. We had antiquated, second-generation weapons, but we could still outfox the world's most modern air forces who had 15th-generation weapons,' Milicevic said."

***

If the US news media got *everything* wrong about the war, what was it doing during the bombing? The following might shed some light on this question (sent along by Sam Smith of prorev.com):

ROBERT FISK, INDEPENDENT, LONDON:

1. [A CNN reporter] "astounded one of his English colleagues after NATO had bombed a narrow road bridge in the Yugoslav village of Varvarin, killing dozens of civilians, many of whom fell to their death in the River Morava. 'That'll teach them not to stand on bridges,' he roared. This was not the kind of language he used on air, of course, where CNN's report on the bridge killings was accompanied by the remark that there had been civilian casualties - according to the Serb authorities, all this when CNN's own crew had been there and filmed the decapitated corpse of the local priest...

2. Two days before NATO bombed the Serb Television headquarters in Belgrade, CNN received a tip from its Atlanta headquarters that the building was to be destroyed. They were told to remove their facilities from the premises at once, which they did. A day later, Serbian Information Minister Aleksander Vucic received a faxed invitation from the Larry King Live show in the US to appear on CNN. They wanted him on air at 2:30 in the morning of 23 April and asked him to arrive at Serb Television half an hour early for make-up. Vucic was late, which was just as well for him since NATO missiles slammed into the building at six minutes past two. The first one exploded in the make-up room where [a] young Serb assistant was burned to death.

CNN calls this all a coincidence, saying that the Larry King show, put out by the entertainment division, did not know of the news department's instruction to its men to leave the Belgrade building."

Yeah, the NATO hit on the make-up room of a multi-floor office building at the exact moment Vucic was scheduled to be there was a coincidence.

Sam sent this along too:

THIS WILL ONLY HURT A LITTLE BIT

UPI: To bring democracy to Kosovo, international officials must act undemocratically in the short run based on lessons learned in implementing peace in Bosnia-Herzegovina, according to the newly appointed Southeastern Europe coordinator for the Organization for Security and Cooperation in Europe... In Kosovo, which is likely to become a protectorate, international officials must create the government institutions, and elections should be postponed, possibly for two years, Barry said. Creating an apolitical judiciary and independent media should be priorities.

- Another "protectorate" which prohibits citizens from voting or even occupying key administrative offices. Surprise, surprise. As a US military official said several months ago about Kosovo: "The model is Bosnia."

War crimes charges filed against Clinton and Cohen

July 12, 1999

The news Brasscheck has been waiting for... and the news you probably haven't heard.

An individual with deep institutional credibility has prepared and filed a detailed case against Clinton and Cohen for the wanton slaughter they directed in the recent US-led assault on Yugoslavia. (From: www.insightmag.com)

It turns out that despite entirely successful manipulation by the US news media - the AP, CNN, the New York Times, the Washington Post, NPR and hundreds of other lesser lights - the facts of the criminal enterprise engaged in by the US in Yugoslavia will not be so easily swept under the carpet.

Since the news of these charges has been pretty much universally censored by the US press, I encourage you to consider making a special effort to forward this dispatch to friends, colleagues, and ethical members of the media.

***

Here are excerpts from an article on the filing published by Insight Magazine and written by James P. Lucier:

"Former chief counsel for the House Watergate committee, Jerome Zeifman, has filed charges before the International Criminal Tribunal seeking the indictment of Clinton and Secretary of Defense William Cohen for alleged war crimes and crimes against humanity. These formal legal documents have been submitted to the [U.N.-established] International Criminal Tribunal for the former Yugoslavia, or ICTY, at The Hague.

Zeifman, a lifelong Democrat whose meticulous preparation of the case against Richard Nixon forced the Republican president out of the White House, is serious. And it raises concerns that, in an age of internationalism and depreciated national sovereignty, the president of the United States, as well as the defense secretary, could be placed in the same defendant's box as Slobodan Milosevic, the indicted Yugoslavian war criminal.

Zeifman tells Insight the proposed indictment specifically incorporates all the charges of war crimes already pending against Milosevic and his henchmen and supplements them with the charges against Clinton and Cohen. Since the "aggressive military attacks" against Serbia and Kosovo were not necessary to defend the United States, the proposal argues, they fall under the category of "non-defensive aggressive wars" as defined and prohibited in the charter of the Nuremberg tribunal in 1945, and since included in the 1947 U.N. Charter and subsequent Geneva conventions on the treatment of civilians during wartime.

In particular, the proposed indictment cites "War Crimes: namely, violations of the laws or customs of war [including] murder, ill-treatment... of civilian population... wanton destruction of cities, towns or villages, or devastation not justified by military necessity. Crimes against Humanity: namely, murder... and other inhumane acts committed against any civilian population, before or during the war."

Zeifman anticipates that (Jimmy) Carter would be called as a witness -- as well as Walter Rockler, a former Nuremberg prosecutor for the United States -- and notes that Carter charged in May that the United States had launched 14,000 missiles and bombs, 4,000 of which were not precision-guided. These included cluster bombs "that have resulted in damage to hospitals, offices and residences of ambassadors, and the senseless and brutal killing of innocent civilians and conscripted troops."

Partial text from the proposed indictment:

CHARGES

1. The Armed Forces of the United States, acting under orders of defendants CLINTON and COHEN have executed a non-defensive aggressive military campaign against former Yugoslavia.

2. Defendants CLINTON and COHEN and others have committed or aided and abetted actions which they knew, or had reason to know, would result in the following:

COUNT 1

The killing, injuring, terrorizing and destruction of the homes of thousands of Serbian and other civilians in former Yugoslavia, including, but not limited to such acts described by former President Carter as...

1. 25,000 sorties and 14,000 missiles and bombs, 4,000 of which were not precision-guided, as of May 1999.

2. The use of antipersonnel cluster bombs that have resulted in damage to hospitals, offices and residences of ambassadors, and the senseless and brutal killing of innocent civilians and conscripted troops; and

3. The use of specific types of cluster bombs that are designed to kill and maim humans and are condemned almost universally by other nations, as are land mines.

COUNT 2

The provocation of the government of former Yugoslavia to continue to increase the murder, terrorization and deportation of Albanian civilians in Kosovo, and such acts as are charged in the May 24, 1999, indictment of Slobodan Milosevic et al., that are described by Bishop Artemios of Kosovo as resulting in the destruction of democracy in Yugoslavia...

Respectfully submitted by Jerome M. Zeifman, Esq., June 8, 1999.

***

[End of dispatches.]

Appendix

Aleksandar Vučić, President of the Republic of Serbia, addresses the 77th Session of the General Assembly of the UN, in New York - September 20, 2022

"Esteemed president of the General Assembly, distinguished Secretary General, excellencies, ladies and gentlemen, it gives me a great honor to address you on behalf of the Republic of Serbia.

Due to limited time, please do not mind if I skip the burden of formality, courtesy words, greetings of those who are present in this room or absent, and instead, speak directly about the essence of what we gather here. I've been so many times in these premises. The seriousness of the present moment obliges me to share difficult, mature words with you.

Everything we are doing here today seems at least relatively impotent and vague. Our words make hollow and empty echoes comparing to the reality we are facing. And that reality is such that no one is listening to anyone here. No one strives towards real agreements into resolving problems. And almost everyone takes care only of their own interests - breaching often, along the way, the basic principles of international law; throwing away the UN Charter, and other documents this organization is founded on.

It is neither fault of Antonio Guterres, nor of anyone from UN, but of those powers who take care of nothing else, but are meeting their own political, economic, and, unfortunately, military goals.

We are witnesses that the age we live in is featured by complexity of the global geopolitical situation. Our general debate is being held in terms of undermined world peace to the extent that has not been seen ever since World War Two, and since the time the United Nations had been founded. Global challenges we are facing are threatening to radically change international security architecture and jeopardize established international legal order.

Such complex times demand a lot of wisdom and unity in order to preserve peace as the absolutely most important heritage woven into the foundations of the United Nations organization. That is why I would like to speak clearly and accurately before you, about five key challenges we are facing today.

Point one, returning to peace and preservation of global stability.

Point two, preservation of territorial integrity and sovereignty of internationally recognized states - members of this organization - as a key principle of international public law and relations between the countries.

Point three, energy security in terms of global crisis.

Point four, financial safety of the poor and developing countries.

And point five, food supply in terms of global supply chains interrupted by war.

Current global developments remind us more and more often that the principle of peaceful resolution of disputes has no alternative. This principle is outstanding today more than ever before. And it is best described in the UN Charter preamble, which reads as follows: To practice tolerance, and live together in peace with one another as good neighbors.

Denial of use of force and peaceful resolution of disputes are the pillars of real stability. But they must be accompanied by principles such as non-selective observance of the UN charter, implementation of mandatory UN Security Council resolutions, and basic principles of the applicable International Public Law.

Point two, preservation of territorial integrity and sovereignty of internationally recognized states members of this organization. Serbia supports territorial integrity of all UN member states, including, of course, territorial integrity of Ukraine. In such a way we behave responsibly and seriously in this renowned institution. Nevertheless, we could hear from many speakers the stories about aggression, and violation of territorial integrity of Ukraine.

Many say that this was the first conflict on European soil after World War Two. But the truth, that the territorial integrity of a country in Europe - Serbia, as a matter of fact, which did not attack any other sovereign country - was violated, is constantly unspoken.

We ask for a clear answer to the question - I've been asking my interlocutors, leaders of many countries, for years - what is the difference between the sovereignty and territorial integrity of Ukraine, and sovereignty and territorial integrity of Serbia, which was grossly violated, and for which you provided international recognition and legitimacy? (At least some of you.)

Nobody has ever provided a rational answer to this question.

Let me remind you: Serbia has not stepped foot on someone else's territory, never ever. Nor has it endangered territorial integrity of a single sovereign state, so that anyone might intervene or carry out aggression against it, the way it was done against Serbia in 1999.

Nevertheless, as I said, it did not prevent 19 [of the] richest NATO countries from attacking a sovereign country, without a decision by the United Nations Security Council.

Signing of the agreement with NATO upon termination of armed conflict, whose provisions envisaged adoption of the UN Security Council resolution 1244, and which confirmed and guaranteed partial sovereignty and full territorial integrity of Serbia, did not prevent many Western countries from unilateral recognition of independence of the so-called Kosovo, and from violating, once again, territorial integrity of our country, and violating the UN Charter and the UN resolution 1244.

Precisely for such developments that Serbia experienced, and that it has been experiencing, I'm convinced that I'm fully entitled to quote, in this place, the words of the great Martin Luther King: injustice anywhere, is a threat to justice everywhere.

These words are carved, like a reminder, but as a warning to all of us. Regardless of the fact that we still feel the consequences of the gross violation of basic provisions of International Public Law, we do not give up on United Nations Foundation principles. We shall keep advocating consistent observance of the principle of inviolability of borders, respect for sovereignty and integrity of all other UN member states.

Despite such a position of ours, men in this room have issues with respecting territorial integrity of Serbia.

You wonder why?

Because they have the power in their hands. And in their eyes, we are small and weak. However, as you could hear, and as you could see, we do have the strength to tell the truth, even here.

Your Excellencies, we owe special gratitude to all those UN member states, and they currently constitute the majority of this assembly, who support territorial integrity of the Republic of Serbia, particularly in the space and territory of Kosovo and Metohija.

It is additionally encouraging that the number of countries who support Serbia's position, increased in the period between two sessions, which is a trend that must continue, because it is of utmost importance to remain loyal to basic principles embedded into the UN Charter, such as the principle of inviolability of borders.

The Republic of Serbia, and I, as its president, search very patiently, and with a lot of goodwill, for compromise regarding Kosovo and Metohija, under the auspices of the European Union and within Belgrade Pristina dialogue.

It is a difficult process. It has been lasting for more than 10 years. But we see no alternative to it.

It is better to negotiate for a hundred years than to wage war for a single day.

I hope that we will reach a mutually acceptable solution based on compromise, because this is the absolutely only way for reaching our goal, which is a long-lasting peace as a prerequisite of prosperous life for Serbs and Albanians, and our entire region.

We have exhausted all other options, and speaking for Serbia, at least, we do not even dream about going back to the paths of conflicts and bloodshed. The Balkan region could not stand another conflict.

I rely on goodwill and understanding from our international partners, because they know well that some earlier decisions by their governments had been bad, and that they had not been acting in favor of the future of our region, and world peace.

Belgrade is running this process under very complex circumstances, with elements of hybrid war and a dirty campaign in part of international community against our country, in different fields. It will be enough just to remind you of the quotes and allegations of world media, that Serbia would attack its neighbors, and that Serbia was a threat to regional stability.

Of course, it has never happened - and it was only one among numerous lies against the Republic of Serbia.

Serbia was featured as a potential destabilizing factor in the region, only to be prevented from telling the truth, that the principle of inviolability of borders must be equally applicable to all.

Serbia was, and it will be, a factor of stability in the entire region. And Serbia, despite many untruths and forgeries, supports (NATO peace accords), territorial integrity of Bosnia and Herzegovina, and integrity of Republika Srpska within Bosnia and Herzegovina.

On the other hand, we are convinced that the nations of the Balkans do have the capacity to continue their lives in the future as friends and partners, with a common vision of membership to the united Europe. I know this well, because we have already surpassed many barriers that had been standing between our nations for years, and that had cost us thousands of lives and wasted future. Serbia and Albania, for example, today, have the closest and the friendliest relationship in the entire several centuries-long common history in the space of the Balkan Peninsula.

It took only clear-headed and pragmatic discussions about our future, not about our past; to talk about how to resolve problems that were bothering our people, or companies, workers, students, and entrepreneurs.

We had discussed a lot and reached by ourselves numerous solutions that have already canceled barriers that existed between us for no rational reasons.

First of all in economy, trade, and flow of people and capital. Serbia, Albania, North Macedonia have been implementing for three years, open Balkan initiative, which has a clear vision to open the region for the people, goods, services, capital and companies, in order to create a space which will be permanently liberated from tensions and conflict.

In addition to [the] unquestionable common economic benefit that this initiative brings, it has a broader dimension.

First of all, in connecting people with different cultures and in promoting diversity, which by all means, contributes to general development of society in this part of Europe. This way, Serbia actually continues contributing to peace, stability, and reconciliation process in the region - whereby it certainly gives significant contribution to global security.

We found the inspiration [in] the respective words of one of the greatest diplomats in history, and the great UN Secretary General, Dag Hammarskjöld - that this organization was not created to take mankind into paradise, but rather to save humanity from hell.

Ladies and gentlemen, the moment we curbed the global pandemic, we have already faced new, unprecedented challenges for the century. While we, as a mankind, take one step at a time, and accelerate technological development, there lies existential problems ahead of us, such as energy security, financial safety of the developing countries, but also distortions in the supply chains of the basic food provisions. Solidarity, which can be necessary in fighting a pandemic, is needed to a far greater extent today, when people's basic necessities for food and energy are endangered.

The Republic of Serbia thinks of its energy security as of the inseparable part of the national security, and as the key prerequisite for the continuation of economic development and progress of our country.

We strive to provide a continuity of energy supply, but we share the concern for current geopolitical challenges that undermine the energy stability in the world and Europe. We remain committed to finding solutions that might have the transformational strength in attempts to reach regional and European energy safety. I would like to underline that the Republic of Serbia managed to preserve continuity in energy supply during the ongoing crisis. Nevertheless, we remain vitally interested in diversifying supply sources, in additional investment in energy infrastructure, but also in faster and more efficient development of capacities based on renewables.

It is precisely at the United Nations where we named the ongoing decade the decade of more sustainable and resilient future, action, and transformation. It has to remain like that, but at a bit faster pace.

Unequal development, but also, financial perils in the developing countries, cause additional social layering and can inevitably bring new antagonisms. Equal development must neither be limited, nor conditioned, either geographically or politically, but it must be provided to all people regardless of (ethnic), racial, cultural, or religious affiliation.

There is another very important challenge ahead, which we must overcome together, and it is finding the most efficient way to avoid consequences of the current international crisis inflicted on global food supply security. Developments are highly alarming, and the reality is such that all of us, with no exceptions, are struck by them.

Growing prices of food and its availability have become an additional problem. The task for all of us is to find operational and efficient solutions that will leave no one behind. It is up to us states, as the most important international subjects, to involve individual and coordination of measures. First of all, by contributing to this noble task at national levels, in order to preserve the most valuable things, human lives, and their dignity.

The topic of this year's general debate warns us [of] the problems of a moment and relatedness of international challenges. Crises we are facing remind us of the importance of open communication.

It does not take much wisdom to conclude that challenges can be successfully overpowered only if their causes are properly observed.

Serbia believes that it is imperative that current challenges must not deepen world divisions in any way. And that already obvious and intentional polarization at a global level should make room to principles of multilateralism.

I would like to underline that the Republic of Serbia take part in collective efforts for reaching sustainable development goals and implementation of the 2030 agenda.

Serbia shares Secretary General's vision and future of global cooperation in a way envisaged by our common agenda, and it strongly supports inclusive networked and efficient multilateralism as the best tool for responding to the most urgent challenges for mankind.

Ladies and gentlemen: multilateralism, collective actions, and common responsibility are irreplaceable elements of our discussion so far. But allow me to underline, the starting point for each such constructive engagement is solidarity.

Finally, I would like to reiterate that the Republic of Serbia will continue being a reliable partner in achieving common goals defined within the UN framework, firmly believing that it is the best path to create a world for us and generations to come. But we must not forget that the United Nations are as strong as we respect commonly harmonized decisions, and documents of this organization.

Once again, I would quote something that we [have] heard 23 times since now, this is the sentence: the only standard we must follow is [the] UN Charter. That's what we heard from everybody. But when we come to the case of the Republic of Serbia, then we saw that 17 out of those 23 that were speaking about [the] UN Charter and UN resolution, violated international public law, and did not obey the rules created and made by the United Nations.

I hope that we'll be able to overcome all these difficulties and to make it equal, the rules and procedures, for everybody in the world.

Otherwise, I don't see the exit at the end of the tunnel.

Anyway, thank you very much for listening to me. And I hope that we'll be able to overcome all the difficulties.

Long live Serbia."

About The Author

Ken McCarthy was one of the early pioneers of the movement to commercialize the Internet in the early 1990s. Time Magazine credits him with being the first person to recognize and articulate the importance of the click-through rate as a key metric for making the Internet commercially viable.

He was also a pioneer of, and in some cases directly initiated, the use of many now-common Internet publishing activities: email marketing (1994), banner advertising (1994), A/B split testing (1996), email auto-responders (1996), blogging (1997), push-button audio content (now known as "podcasting") (2002), online video (2005), and mobile marketing (2008).

Related Titles from Brasscheck Press
Available on Amazon.com

The Nuremberg Code: 75th Anniversary Commemorative Edition

With a moving introduction by Holocaust survivor Vera Sharav, this 75th Anniversary Commemorative Edition of the Nuremberg Code features translations of the original text in 11 languages.

A concise and essential document on the subject of patient rights, drafted in response to many heinous abuses by doctors, nurses, and public health officials during the Nazi regime.

Death, Resurrection, and the Spirit of New Orleans Jazz on the Tube Conversations

When New Orleans was devastated in 2005 by the failure of the U.S. Army Corps of Engineers levee system many thought the city was finished.

This book documents how the people of New Orleans led by the city's beloved musicians and culture bearers defied all predictions and brought the city back.

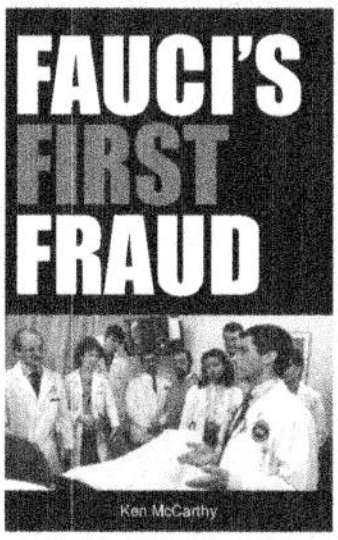

Fauci's First Fraud and the Foundation of Medical Totalitarianism

Forty years before the global COVID panic, U.S. federal bureaucracies like the CDC and NIAID were having trouble justifying their budgets because of the dramatic decline of deaths from infectious diseases.

The solution: The creation of a propaganda machine that successfully both floods the news media with hysterically-tinged reports of biological doom while simultaneously shouting down all rational scientific and medical discussion.

Coming 2024

The Nuremberg Code and its Modern Enemies

Where did respect for the Nuremberg Code go?

In the middle of the COVID Panic, the 75th anniversary of the Nuremberg Code (2022) came and went without recognition or even mention from anyone in the medical ethics profession.

Meanwhile, a cottage industry of "reporters" sprung up producing a stream of articles about how the Code was out of date, not legally binding, and does not apply to COVID vaccines. This book answers the question, "What happened and why?"

Brasscheck.com

In-depth common-sense online reporting since 1997

Printed in Great Britain
by Amazon

38308685R00178